# SPSS

# SPSS® for Windows™ CHAID™ Release 6.0

Jay Magidson / SPSS Inc.

SPSS Inc.
444 N. Michigan Avenue
Chicago, Illinois 60611
Tel: (312) 329-2400
Fax: (312) 329-3668

SPSS Federal Systems (U.S.)
SPSS Argentina srl.
SPSS Asia Pacific Pte. Ltd.
SPSS Australasia Pty. Ltd.
SPSS Belgium
SPSS Benelux BV
SPSS Central and Eastern Europe
SPSS France SARL
SPSS Germany
SPSS Hellas SA
SPSS Hispanoportuguesa S.L.
SPSS Ireland
SPSS Israel Ltd.
SPSS Italia srl
SPSS Japan Inc.
SPSS Korea
SPSS Latin America
SPSS Malaysia Sdn Bhd
SPSS Mexico SA de CV
SPSS Middle East and Africa
SPSS Scandinavia AB
SPSS Schweiz AG
SPSS Singapore Pte. Ltd.
SPSS UK Ltd.

For more information about SPSS® software products, please write or call

Marketing Department
SPSS Inc.
444 North Michigan Avenue
Chicago, IL 60611
Tel: (312) 329-2400
Fax: (312) 329-3668



SPSS® for Windows™: CHAID™, Release 6.0

Printed in the United States of America.



5 6 7 8 9 0    96

ISBN 0-13-178849-3

# Preface

CHAID™ for Windows™ Release 6 represents the third generation of CHAID analysis software. You can display your results simultaneously in the form of an intuitive tree diagram, crosstabulations, and a gains chart summary of the analysis. You can treat your dependent variable as nominal or ordinal, and you can combine categories of a predictor variable in any way. CHAID also has a new maximum-likelihood calibration method for estimating category scores for an ordinal dependent variable when some or all of the scores are unknown.

In addition to CHAID's unique manner of performing exploratory segmentation analysis, the program performs several confirmatory analyses and other specialized analyses, such as the assessment of clinical trials or other treatment effects (see Chapter 5). These new capabilities, which are based on recent advances in maximum-likelihood methodology (Goodman, 1991), are not available in any other program.

CHAID for Windows Release 6 is a stand-alone program developed by Statistical Innovations Inc. The program accepts data directly from an ASCII data file or a binary data file. Alternatively, data, variable names, and value labels may be imported from any system file saved by SPSS PC+ (version 2 or later). CHAID can be invoked directly from Windows or from SPSS for Windows. CHAID for Windows Release 6 is marketed, distributed, and supported exclusively by SPSS Inc. as part of the SPSS family of statistical programs.

## Acknowledgements

The magazine subscription data set that accompanies the software is used throughout this manual for purposes of illustration. I wish to thank the R.L. Polk company for making this data available.

I also wish to thank J. Alexander Ahlstrom for his assistance in the design and development of the program, Frank Derrick for his diligent efforts in developing this manual, coordinating the beta test sites and providing helpful comments, and the numerous users for their helpful comments regarding earlier versions of the program.

Specifically, I'd like to single out Graham Barlow of Raymead Consulting (U.K.), John Miglautsch of Miglautsch Marketing, Mike Crump and David Vonesh of Strategy Research & Re-engineering, and Peter Taves of the Growth Strategies Group for helpful comments and recommendations. Finally, I'd like to thank Alex Karpovsky for his important contributions.

Jay Magidson,
Belmont, Massachusetts
June 1993

## About This Manual

Chapter 2 through Chapter 5 introduce the basic ideas of CHAID segmentation modeling and provide several examples using data that accompany the software. Each example demonstrates a major feature of the program. Hands-on tutorials in these chapters will help you get up and running quickly.

Chapter 6 describes all CHAID menus and commands. Technical appendices are provided for advanced users who want to know more about statistics that form the basis of CHAID.

## Contacting SPSS Inc.

If you would like to be on our mailing list, contact one of our offices below. We will send you a copy of our newsletter and let you know about SPSS Inc. activities in your area.


**SPSS Inc.**
Chicago, Illinois, U.S.A.
Tel: 1.312.329.2400
Fax: 1.312.329.3668
Customer Service:
1.800.521.1337
Sales:
1.800.543.2185
sales@spss.com
Training:
1-800-543-6607
Technical Support:
1.312.329.3410
support@spss.com

**SPSS Federal Systems**
Arlington, Virginia, U.S.A.
Tel: 1.703.527.6777
Fax: 1.703.527.6866

**SPSS Argentina srl.**
Buenos Aires, Argentina
Tel: +541.816.4086
Fax: +541.814.5030

**SPSS Asia Pacific Pte. Ltd.**
Singapore, Singapore
Tel: +65.3922.738
Fax: +65.3922.739

**SPSS Australasia Pty. Ltd.**
Sydney, Australia
Tel: +61.2.9954.5660
Fax: +61.2.9954.5616

**SPSS Belgium**
Heverlee, Belgium
Tel: +32.162.389.82
Fax: +32.1620.0888

**SPSS Benelux BV**
Gorinchem, The Netherlands
Tel: +31.183.636711
Fax: +31.183.635839

**SPSS Central and Eastern Europe**
Woking, Surrey, U.K.
Tel: +44.(0)1483.719200
Fax: +44.(0)1483.719290

**SPSS France SARL**
Boulogne, France
Tel: +33.1.4699.9670
Fax: +33.1.4684.0180

**SPSS Germany**
Munich, Germany
Tel: +49.89.4890740
Fax: +49.89.4483115

**SPSS Hellas SA**
Athens, Greece
Tel: +30.1.7251925
Fax: +30.1.7249124

**SPSS Hispanoportuguesa S.L.**
Madrid, Spain
Tel: +34.1.547.3703
Fax: +34.1.548.1346

**SPSS Ireland**
Dublin, Ireland
Tel: +353.1.66.13788
Fax: +353.1.661.5200

**SPSS Israel Ltd.**
Herzlia, Israel
Tel: +972.9.598900
Fax: +972.9.598903

**SPSS Italia srl**
Bologna, Italy
Tel: +39.51.252573
Fax: +39.51.253285

**SPSS Japan Inc.**
Tokyo, Japan
Tel: +81.3.5474.0341
Fax: +81.3.5474.2678

**SPSS Korea**
Seoul, Korea
Tel: +82.2.552.9415
Fax: +82.2.539.0136

**SPSS Latin America**
Chicago, Illinois, U.S.A.
Tel: 1.312.494.3226
Fax: 1.312. 494.3227

**SPSS Malaysia Sdn Bhd**
Kuala Lumpur, Malaysia
Tel: +60.3.2387541
Fax: +60.3.2387560

**SPSS Mexico SA de CV**
Mexico DF, Mexico
Tel: +52.5.575.3091
Fax: +52.5.575.3094

**SPSS Middle East and Africa**
Woking, Surrey, U.K.
Tel: +44.(0)1483.719200
Fax: +44.(0)1483.719290

**SPSS Scandinavia AB**
Stockholm, Sweden
Tel: +46.8.102610
Fax: +46.8.102550

**SPSS Schweiz AG**
Zurich, Switzerland
Tel: +41.1.201.0930
Fax: +41.1.201.0921

**SPSS Singapore Pte. Ltd.**
Singapore, Singapore
Tel: +65.2991238
Fax: +65.2990849

**SPSS UK Ltd.**
Woking, Surrey, U.K.
Tel: +44.(0)1483.719200
Fax: +44.(0)1483.719290

# Contents

# 1 Installing CHAID for Windows

These instructions tell you how to install your CHAID for Windows software on a hard disk. You will need one 5.25-inch distribution diskette (high density) or one 3.5-inch diskette, CH1, to complete the installation. If you are installing to a network see the installation instructions included with the network licensed software.

## System Requirements

To install and run CHAID for Windows, the minimum equipment you will need includes:

- Windows 3.1 installed, running in 386 enhanced mode.*
- A disk drive that can read high-density 3.5-inch or 5.25-inch diskettes.
- A hard disk with at least 1MB of free space.
- A VGA monitor and adapter set to 640 x 480 graphics resolution.
- A mouse compatible with Windows 3.1.

The following upgrade will improve performance and is therefore strongly recommended:

- A math coprocessor. Statistics will be tabulated more quickly if a math coprocessor is present.

*Windows in 386 enhanced mode implies 386 or better and 2MB of RAM.

## Installation Procedure

After making sure that your computer is suitable for CHAID for Windows, follow these steps to install the program:

1. Insert the 5.25-inch diskette or the 3.5-inch diskette CH1 in the A or B drive.
2. Open the File menu on the Windows Program Manager screen.
3. Select Run. Windows displays the Run dialog box, as shown in Figure 1.1.

**Figure 1.1 Run dialog box**

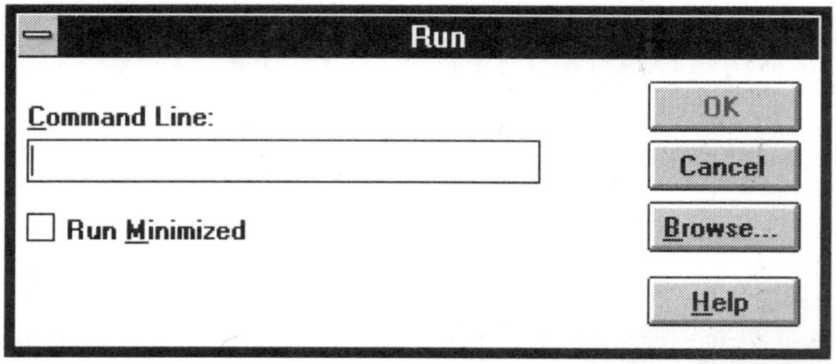


4. Type `a:setup` or `b:setup`, depending on which drive the installation diskette is in, and click on OK. CHAID now starts its installation program.

   If this is the first time CHAID has been installed, you will be prompted for your name and organization name.

5. When asked if you want to continue the setup, click on Continue. You will be asked to confirm the drive and directory where you wish to install CHAID. To accept the default, *c:\chaidwin*, click on Continue.

   When the installation is finished, a CHAID icon is displayed on the Windows Program Manager screen. (For instructions on how to start CHAID, see Chapter 3.) Installation also registers CHAID in the Registration Database so that if you use SPSS for Windows, SPSS CHAID will appear on the Statistics menu when you restart SPSS.

# 2 Overview of CHAID

Imagine that you are a direct marketer who sells subscriptions to a magazine. To maximize your profits, you want to identify household segments that, based on previous promotions, are most likely to respond to a magazine promotion. Or, suppose that you are a health care professional who wants to identify population segments at the greatest risk for heart disease. CHAID (Chi-squared Automatic Interaction Detector) performs **segmentation modeling**, a relatively new statistical application that is useful in any situation in which your overall goal is to divide a population into segments that differ with respect to a designated criterion.

CHAID divides a population into two or more distinct groups based on categories of the "best" predictor of a dependent variable. It then splits each of these groups into smaller subgroups based on other predictor variables. This splitting process continues until no more statistically significant predictors can be found (or until some other stopping rule is met). CHAID displays the final subgroups (**segments**) on an easy-to-understand tree diagram.

The segments that CHAID derives are **mutually exclusive** and **exhaustive**. That is, segments do not overlap, and each population unit (case) is contained in exactly one segment. In addition, since segments are defined by combinations of predictor variables, you can easily classify each case into its appropriate segment simply by knowing the categories of these predictors.

## A CHAID Analysis

Let's examine a CHAID analysis for a direct marketing promotion used to encourage people to subscribe to a magazine. (The data are in the SPSS data file *subscrib.sav* that is included on your installation disk.) Households that were sent the promotion were categorized as paid responders, unpaid responders, or nonresponders. Paid responders were households that returned a mail form, checked off the item that they would like to subscribe to the magazine, and later paid for the subscription. Unpaid responders were households that returned the form and checked off the item that they would like to subscribe to the magazine, but then canceled their subscriptions prior to paying. Nonresponders were all others (that is, all households that did not request a subscription).

For this initial example, the dependent variable is *resp2* (coded 1 for paid and unpaid responders and 2 for nonresponders). Predictor variables include *age* (age of head of household), *gender* (sex of head of household), *kids* (presence of children), *income* (household income), *bankcard* (presence of a bankcard), *hhsize* (number of persons in the household), and *occup* (occupational status of the head of household). As in any CHAID analysis, the dependent variable and the predictor variables are categorical. Values of a categorical variable represent distinct groups. See "Categorical Variable" on p. 8 for more information. For a complete description of the variables in *subscrib.sav*, see Appendix C.

## A Tree Diagram

A CHAID analysis begins by dividing the population into two or more distinct groups based on the categories of the best predictor. It then splits these groups into smaller subgroups. CHAID displays segmentation results in the form of a tree diagram whose branches (nodes) correspond to the groups. As each of these groups is split further into smaller subgroups, the tree spawns additional nodes. At any point in a CHAID analysis, the tree diagram shows the current state of the analysis. Figure 2.1 is a tree diagram based on an analysis of the magazine subscription data set, in which *resp2* is the dependent variable. The following figure is annotated to show depth levels.

**Figure 2.1 Tree diagram for magazine subscription data set**

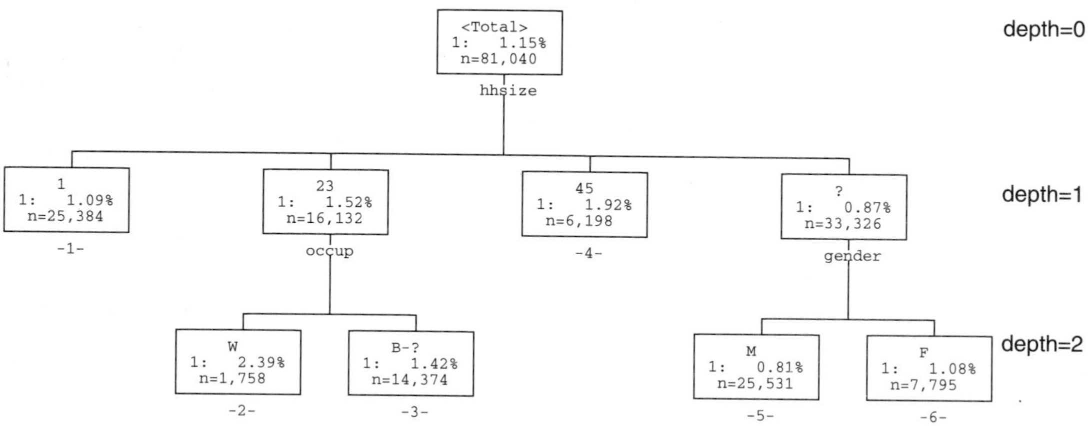


Each node on the tree diagram represents a population subgroup. The three rows of information in each node describe the subgroup. The first row contains a symbol that identifies the particular category (or categories) that defines the subgroup (for an SPSS data file, these symbols are the actual category values or, if value labels are defined, the first character of the value label). The second row contains a summary statistic for the subgroup, based on values of the dependent variable. For this example, the summary statistic in each node is the percentage of cases that responded to the mail promotion (the "1:" that precedes the percentage indicates that the percentage of cases coded 1 for the dependent variable is shown). The final row contains the subgroup size for the node.

For example, look at the initial node (**root node** or **parent node**) of the tree, which represents the total sample. The second row, 1: 1.15%, indicates that 1.15% of the households in the sample responded to the mailing. This percentage is the overall response rate for the mailing. The final row tells you that the promotion was mailed to 81,040 households.

The root node is the parent of four **child nodes**. The child nodes are formed by the categories of *hhsize*, the best predictor of whether or not a household responded to the promotion. The first *hhsize* node (the leftmost node in Figure 2.1), which contains the category symbol 1, represents one-person households. The response rate was 1.09% for the 25,384 one-person households. Similarly, the node identified by the symbol 23 represents two- and three-person households in the sample. For the 16,132 households in this group, the response rate was 1.52%. CHAID has also split *hhsize* into two additional subgroups, four- and five-person households and households having an unknown number of persons. The "unknown" category is coded as a question mark (?). Note that the sample sizes for the *hhsize* nodes sum to the total sample size shown in the parent node (25,384 + 16,132 + 6,198 +33,326 = 81,040).

At the next level of the tree, you can see that CHAID further split two- and three-person households into two smaller subgroups, one containing white-collar households and the other containing households headed by blue-collar workers and households in which the occupation of the head of household is unknown. CHAID performed this split because the response rates for these two subgroups are significantly different. The two sample sizes of the *occup* nodes (1,758 and 14,374) sum to the sample size of their parent node, two- and three-person households (16,132). CHAID also split households having an unknown number of persons into households headed by males and households headed by females.

The terminal nodes of the tree are the **final segments**, which are identified by a dashed number (for example, segment 1 is identified as –1–). Table 2.1 describes the final segments for our direct marketing example. This initial analysis was limited to a depth of two using the Depth Limit option. No further splits were performed on segment 1 or 4, because no predictors were statistically significant.

**Table 2.1 Segment descriptions**

| Segment | Description | Response rate |
|---|---|---|
| 1 | One-person households | 1.09% |
| 2 | Two- or three-person households in which the head of household is a white-collar worker | 2.39% |
| 3 | Two- or three-person households in which the head of household is not a white-collar worker | 1.42% |
| 4 | Households containing four or five persons | 1.92% |
| 5 | Number of persons in household is unknown and head of household is male | 0.81% |
| 6 | Number of persons in household is unknown and head of household is female | 1.08% |

## Category Merging

CHAID merges categories of a predictor variable that are not significantly different. This merging procedure, combined with the splitting algorithm, ensures that cases in the same segment are homogeneous with respect to the segmentation criterion, while cases in different segments tend to be heterogeneous with respect to the segmentation criterion. For example, while *hhsize* originally had six categories, CHAID merged categories whose response rates were statistically indistinguishable. For example, two- and three-person households were merged into a single joint category, and four-person households were combined with households containing five or more persons. Thus, after merging, household size contains four categories.

## Interpreting the Results

Looking at the tree diagram in Figure 2.1, you can see that segment 2 had the highest response rate (2.39%) of any segment. Thus, if you wanted to target only the highest responding households in future promotions, you would send the promotional materials to two- or three-person households in which the head of the household has a white-collar occupation. The lowest responding segment was segment 5, which consists of households of unknown size in which the head of household is male. The response rate for this segment (0.81%) was significantly below the overall response rate of 1.15%.

## Segments versus Clusters

While both CHAID and traditional cluster analysis divide a population into subgroups, only CHAID uses a dependent variable as a criterion for forming the subgroups. (Statistical significance between the dependent variable and the predictors drives CHAID's segmentation algorithm.) Thus, while CHAID segments are derived to predict a dependent variable, clusters may not be predictive. For example, segment 2, which is predicted to be most likely to respond, will tend to have a higher rate of response than any cluster of equal size obtained in a traditional cluster analysis.

Another difference between clusters and segments is that clusters generally are not defined as explicit functions of the predictors. Thus, the results of a cluster analysis cannot be used easily to classify a new sample into clusters. Segmentation analysis is a more appropriate technique than cluster analysis when your goal is to produce clusters that predict some dependent variable criterion, or to apply classifications to another sample.

## Other Uses of CHAID

While the primary goal of CHAID is segmentation analysis, you can also use CHAID to address other statistical issues. For example, CHAID can be used in each of the following scenarios:

- A statistician wants to know what interaction effects to include in a logistic regression analysis.
- A biomedical researcher wants to understand how risk factors for heart disease interact with each other.
- A marketing researcher wishes to scan through hundreds of crosstabulations and select those that are most statistically significant.
- The same marketing researcher wants to simplify the selected crosstabulations by combining categories that don't differ significantly.
- A psychometrician wishes to develop a quantitative scale for an ordinal variable.
- A new database manager suspects that the system she has inherited is loaded down with useless data. She wants to know which of several hundred variables she can safely eliminate.
- A TV network wishes to display election results in terms of the most relevant demographic groupings.

## Components of a CHAID Analysis

A CHAID analysis has the following basic components:

- One or more predictor variables whose values are used to define the segments. You can use any type of categorical predictor variable, including demographic, lifestyle, psychographic, and behavioral variables. Each predictor can contain up to 31 categories.
- The criterion for building the segmentation model. This criterion is controlled by the choice of the dependent variable (which must be categorical), the method of analysis (nominal or ordinal), and, if the ordinal method is selected, category scores. The dependent variable can contain up to 31 categories.
- Settings for the various CHAID parameters.

# Types of Variables

This section defines the term "categorical variable" and describes the various types of variables that may be used in a CHAID analysis. In addition to the analysis variables, CHAID also allows you to use a frequency variable and a weight variable. You can use these variables to reduce the size of your data file, which will help speed up the analysis.

## Categorical Variable

**Categorical variables** differ from **continuous variables** in that they are not measured in a continuous fashion but are classified into distinct groups. You can convert continuous variables to categorical variables by grouping adjacent values. For example, for the previous analysis, the continuous variable *age* was grouped into the following categories: 18 through 24, 25 through 34, 35 through 44, 45 through 54, 55 through 64, and all ages greater than 64.

Categorical variables may be nominal or ordinal. Categories of a **nominal variable** differ in kind rather than in degree, so they have no natural ordering. For example, it may not make sense to order occupational categories such as "white collar," "blue collar," "other," and "unknown." **Ordinal variables** have known or unknown numeric scores associated with their categories. It makes sense to compute the mean (average score) for an ordinal variable, but not for a nominal variable.

If the dependent variable is nominal, the segmentation criterion is based on the probability distribution of the dependent variable. If the dependent variable is ordinal, the criterion is the mean, or expected value, of the specified category scores.

In a CHAID analysis, the dependent variable and each predictor can contain up to 31 categories. If any of your variables contains more than 31 categories, you must recode it prior to a CHAID analysis, or it will be omitted from the analysis.

## Frequency Variable

The magazine subscription data set illustrates use of a **frequency variable**, which represents the total number of observations that falls in a particular cell. Rather than creating a data set that contains 81,040 records—one record for each household mailed—we created one record for each cell in the multi-way table formed by all of the dependent and predictor variables.

For example, Table 2.2 shows a partial listing of the magazine subscription data set. Each row contains cases with a particular combination of values for the variables in the file (the table shows actual category codes instead of value labels). The frequency variable (*freq*) indicates how many cases each record represents. Thus, the first row in the table contains 14 cases and the second row contains 4 cases.

**Table 2.2 Sample of data in magazine subscription data set**

| age | gender | kids | income | bankcard | hhsize | occup | resp3 | resp2 | freq |
|---|---|---|---|---|---|---|---|---|---|
| 3 | 1 | 1 | 8 | 2 | 3 | 1 | 3 | 2 | 14 |
| 3 | 1 | 1 | 8 | 2 | 3 | 2 | 3 | 2 | 4 |
| 3 | 1 | 1 | 8 | 2 | 3 | 3 | 3 | 2 | 17 |
| 3 | 1 | 1 | 8 | 2 | 3 | 4 | 3 | 2 | 13 |
| 3 | 1 | 1 | 8 | 2 | 4 | 1 | 3 | 2 | 33 |
| 3 | 1 | 1 | 8 | 2 | 4 | 2 | 3 | 2 | 19 |
| 3 | 1 | 1 | 8 | 2 | 4 | 3 | 3 | 2 | 1 |
| 3 | 1 | 1 | 8 | 2 | 4 | 3 | 3 | 2 | 29 |
| 3 | 1 | 1 | 8 | 2 | 4 | 4 | 3 | 2 | 7 |
| 3 | 1 | 1 | 8 | 2 | 5 | 1 | 2 | 1 | 1 |

The sum of the values for a frequency variable should always be equal to the total number of observations in the sample.

Using a frequency variable will reduce the size of your data file when the number of observations exceeds the number of non-empty cells in the multi-way table. However, the output and statistics are the same whether you use a frequency variable or case-by-case data.

**SPSS Weight Variable.** SPSS allows you to weight cases. The SPSS weight variable determines the number of times each case is included in an analysis, which is exactly what the CHAID frequency variable does. If you want your CHAID analysis to match your SPSS analyses and you are using a weight variable in your SPSS data file, you should use that variable as your CHAID frequency variable.

## Weight Variable

The use of a weight variable gives unequal treatment to the cases in a data set. When a **weight variable** is used, the contribution of a case in the analysis is weighted in proportion to the population units that the case represents in the sample. For example, suppose that in a direct marketing promotion, 10,000 households respond and 1,000,000 households do not respond. To reduce the size of the data file, you might include all of the responders, but only a 1% sample (10,000) of the nonresponders. You can do this if you define a weight variable equal to 1 for responders and 100 for nonresponders.

By default, the weighted loglinear modeling (WLM) algorithm is employed whenever a weight variable is specified. In the preceding example in which only nonresponders are sampled (the sample being 10,000 of the total 1,000,000 nonresponders), the statistics and output will be identical whether or not WLM is used. With more complicated weighting schemes, such as those resulting from complex sampling designs, the WLM algorithm should always be used (Clogg & Eliasin, 1987; Magidson, 1987). For further details on the WLM option, see Appendix B.

If you use a frequency variable and a weight variable, you can compute the weight variable as an average cell weight or the total weighted count for each cell (SPSS for Windows CHAID will accept either type of weight variable). If no frequency variable is used, the weight variable represents the total weighted count corresponding to a particular observation in the analysis sample.

Frequency and weight variables serve different functions. If a weight variable is mistakenly specified to be a frequency variable, or vice versa, the resulting CHAID analysis will be incorrect.

## Predictor Variable

Before beginning a CHAID analysis, you should classify each predictor that contains at least three categories as monotonic, free, or float. This choice affects CHAID's category-merging algorithm and calculation of significance levels. You do not need to classify **dichotomous predictors** (predictors containing only two categories), since they are treated the same way by CHAID whether they are classified as monotonic, free, or float.

Categories of a monotonic variable can be combined only if they are adjacent to each other. Generally, you should treat **ordinal predictors** (predictors whose categories contain a natural ordering) as monotonic. For example, income categories would usually be considered as ordinal and treated as monotonic.

Float variables are treated as monotonic except that the final category (which often represents missing values) is allowed to combine with any other category. For example, in the magazine subscription data, the predictor *age* would normally be treated as monotonic except that the final category represents "unknown." Thus, *age* is defined as a float variable. Since CHAID orders the categories of a variable according to their values, the final category is the category having the highest value. When CHAID analyzes an SPSS data file, the final category is the one assigned an SPSS missing value. For further details regarding the treatment of missing values, see the discussion below.

CHAID can combine categories of free variables whether or not the categories are adjacent to each other. **Nominal variables** (variables whose categories contain no natural ordering) should always be treated as free. For example, we defined *occup* as a free variable.

You should not hastily define all predictors as free, since this will understate the significance of predictors that could be defined as float or monotonic. Moreover, computation time for a free predictor increases exponentially as its categories increase in number. By default, CHAID treats predictors as monotonic unless the data file is an SPSS data file and one or more of the categories have an SPSS missing-value setting. In this case, the default setting is float, with the missing-value categories being grouped into a single float category.

### Predictor Variables and Missing Values

Missing predictor values are treated like any other predictor categories in CHAID. (You can omit missing dependent variable categories, but not missing predictor values, from within CHAID.) Ordinarily, you should define predictors containing one or more missing-value categories as free variables or float variables. The Float option is similar to imputation, since the float category is merged with (and, hence, takes on the characteristics of) the category with which it shares the most similar distribution of the dependent variable.

### Probability Values and the "Best" Predictor

At each stage in the analysis, CHAID splits the tree on the predictor variable having the lowest probability value, or *p* value, as long as the *p* value is less than the significance level (0.05 by default). The *p* value represents the probability that the observed sample relationship between a predictor and the dependent variable would occur if the two variables were statistically unrelated, or independent. For example, a *p* value of 0.05 means that the observed relationship between the predictor and the dependent variable would occur only 5% of the time if the variables were independent. Thus, the predictor with the lowest *p* value is the one that is least likely to be unrelated to the dependent variable.

## Dependent Variable

The dependent variable in a CHAID analysis can be dichotomous or polytomous. A **dichotomous variable** has two categories, which distinguish between cases that have some trait of interest and cases that don't. Table 2.3 shows some examples of dichotomous dependent variables.

**Table 2.3 Dichotomous variables**

| Variable | Categories |
|---|---|
| response | responder, nonresponder |
| credit risk | good, bad |
| disease | present, absent |
| injury | severe, mild |

In our initial analysis of the magazine subscription data, our dependent variable (*resp2*) distinguished only between households that requested a subscription and those that did not. We ignored an important distinction among those who requested a subscription: Some of the responders paid for their subscription and some did not. Those who did not pay received a sample issue and several more mailings that encouraged them to pay their invoice. More money was spent and lost on responders who did not pay than on those who did not request a subscription.

CHAID segmentation analyses can also be performed on dependent variables that have more than two categories (**polytomous variables**). For example, the responder category of *resp2* may be divided into two groups: those responders who subsequently paid and those who canceled prior to paying. The magazine subscription data set contains a trichotomous variable *resp3* with two categories of responders (paid responders and unpaid responders) and a nonresponder category. Using the *resp3* variable leads us naturally to some method of weighing the relative costs or consequences of the different categories of that variable. This information can be read into CHAID as category scores. (Chapter 5 gives an example of an analysis of *resp3* that uses category scores.)

The dependent variable, whether dichotomous or polytomous, may be treated by CHAID as either nominal or ordinal. If a polytomous variable is treated as ordinal, category scores are used to order the categories and provide a measure of relative distance between them. You can provide the scores, or they can be derived using maximum-likelihood calibration or estimation. The analysis of a dichotomous dependent variable results in the same segmentation whether the nominal or ordinal method is used.

## Dependent Variable and Missing Values

If a dependent variable has a missing category, this category will be counted as part of the total population during the scan process but will not be used in the analysis unless specified by the user. For example, if your data set contains 1000 records, of which 100 had a missing value for the dependent variable, then a correct scan will contain 1000 observations, of which 900 will be used in your analysis (the root tree node will contain n = 900).

To include the missing category, you must assign it a unique score. For example, if you were running a nominal analysis and your dependent variable had four categories plus the missing category, you would open the Method menu, select Nominal, and then assign a unique score to the missing category, which is represented by a period (.). For more information regarding the assigning of scores, see "Method Menu" on p. 109 in Chapter 6.

# 3 Beginning CHAID Analysis

This chapter contains a tutorial that will help you become familiar with the basic features of CHAID. It demonstrates how to obtain the tree diagram shown in the previous chapter and how to obtain supplementary output, including crosstabulations, frequencies, and gains charts.

## How to Obtain a Tree Diagram

The first part of the tutorial shows you how to obtain a tree diagram for the magazine subscription data. You will invoke CHAID, select dependent and predictor variables, set technical parameters for the analysis, generate the tree, and control display options.

### Invoking CHAID

You can invoke CHAID independently or from within SPSS for Windows. To invoke CHAID independently and open the magazine subscription data file:

1. Double click on the CHAID icon.
2. Open the File menu and select New....

CHAID places you into the Select New Data to Analyze dialog box, as shown in Figure 3.1. A list of all files in the current directory with *.sav, .sys,* or *.por* extensions appears in the selection box.

**Figure 3.1 Select New Data to Analyze dialog box**

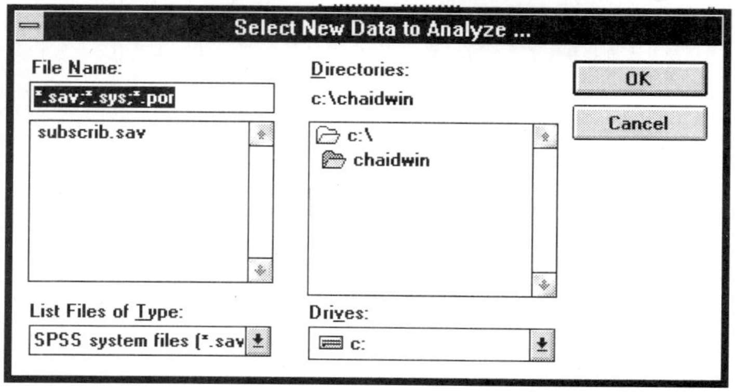


❸ Highlight *subscrib.sav* and click on OK to open the Assign Variables dialog box, as shown in Figure 3.2. The variables in *subscrib.sav* will be listed in the Variables box.

**Figure 3.2 Assign Variables dialog box**

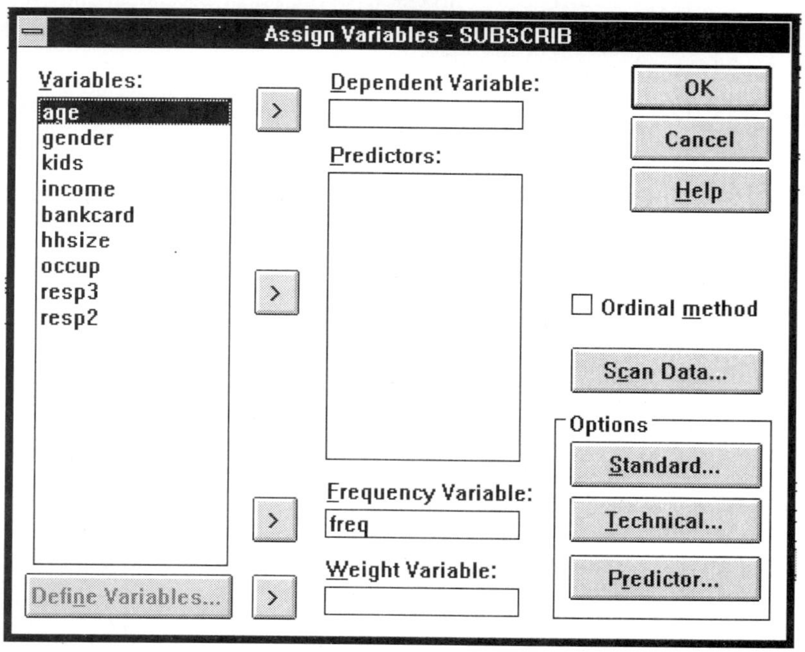


Alternatively, to execute CHAID from within SPSS for Windows:

1. Open SPSS for Windows if you are not already in that program.
2. Open the data file *subscrib.sav* found in the *c:\chaidwin* directory.
3. Open the Statistics menu and select SPSS CHAID.... This opens CHAID and displays the Assign Variables dialog box, shown above in Figure 3.2. The variables in your working data file *(subscrib.sav)* will be listed in the Variables box. From here the analysis proceeds exactly as though you had opened CHAID independently.

## Selecting the Dependent Variable

For this analysis, the dichotomous variable *resp2* will be the dependent variable. To select the dependent variable:

1. Click on *resp2* in the Variables box.
2. Click on the right arrow key next to the Dependent variable box.

The selected dependent variable, *resp2*, now appears in the Dependent Variable box. (If you mistakenly select a variable other than *resp2* as the dependent variable, click on that variable in the Dependent Variable box, and then click on the reverse arrow key to return it to the Variables box.)

## Defining the Predictor Variables

Next, we'll:

- Select the predictor variables.
- Tell CHAID how to treat our predictors when combining categories.
- Change a category symbol and label defined in the SPSS system file.

### Selecting Predictor Variables

To select the predictor variables:

1. Click and drag to highlight *age*, *gender, kids, income, bankcard, hhsize*, and *occup* in the Variables box.
2. Click on the arrow key next to the Predictors box. The variables will now appear in the Predictors box.

To deselect any variable mistakenly selected as a predictor:

1. Highlight the variable name.
2. Click on the reverse arrow key.

## Selecting the Frequency Variable

Our SPSS data file contains a weight variable, *freq*, which is equivalent to the CHAID frequency variable (see “Frequency Variable” on p. 8 in Chapter 2 for more details). Because this was declared as the weight variable when the SPSS file was saved, CHAID automatically assigns it as the frequency variable. It appears in the Frequency Variable box. If this variable had not been declared as the weight variable, you would need to move it into the Frequency Variable box at this time.

## Predictor Types

The Predictors command is used to tell CHAID the method for merging categories of a predictor.

To set the predictor type for *age*:

1. Click on Predictor... to open the Predictor Options dialog box.
2. Click on *age* to highlight it and then click on Float in the Change Combine Type group.
3. Set the predictor types for the remaining predictors. Define *hhsize* as a float variable and *occup* as a free variable, as shown in Figure 3.3.

**Figure 3.3 Predictor Options dialog box**

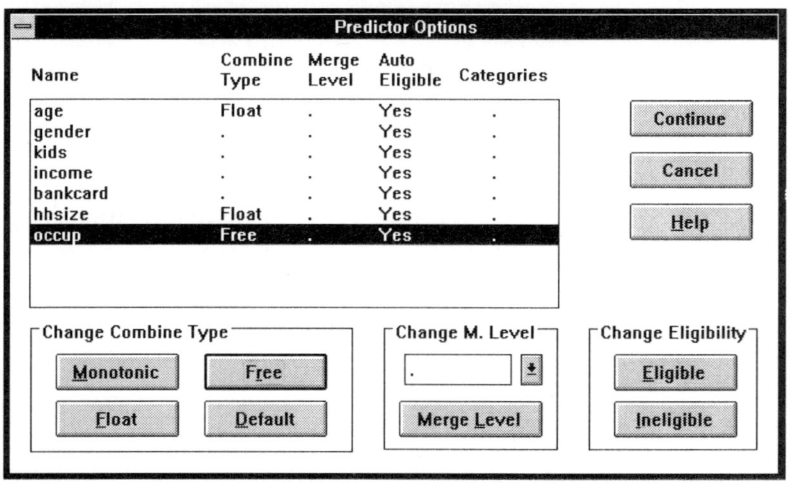


4. The remaining predictors default to monotonic. (The type is monotonic if the Combine Type column contains either Monotonic or a blank.)

5. Click on Continue to return to the Assign Variables dialog box. (See "Predictor Variable" on p. 10 in Chapter 2 for more information on predictor combine types.)

### Setting Standard Options

Standard options control the operation of the segmentation algorithm, including the stopping rule and the minimum segment size.

To set standard options for the analysis:

1. Click on Standard... to open the Standard Options dialog box, as shown in Figure 3.4.

**Figure 3.4 Standard Options dialog box**

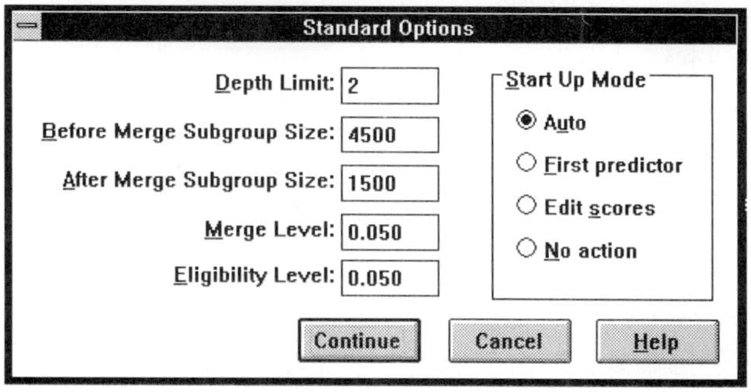


2. Double-click on the Depth Limit text box and enter 2 to set the analysis depth limit at 2. This tells CHAID that the tree should expand to no more than two levels deep.
3. Next, double-click on the Before merge subgroup size text box and enter 4500. This tells CHAID not to split any group that has fewer than 4500 households.
4. Next, double-click on the After merge subgroup size text box and enter 1500. This tells CHAID not to split any group into a subgroup of fewer than 1500 households.
5. Next, click on Auto in the Start Up Mode box to have CHAID run the analysis automatically. (For this analysis, we will leave the rest of the standard options at their default settings.)
6. Click on Continue to return to the Assign Variables dialog box.

## Scanning the Data File

Now that you have set your analysis options, CHAID is ready to scan the data.

To tell CHAID to scan the file:

1. Click on Scan Data.... (If you do not select Scan Data ... before beginning an analysis, CHAID automatically performs a scan before the analysis is begun.)

   Before CHAID scans the data, the Save As dialog box appears, as shown in Figure 3.5. This dialog box is used to specify a filename for the output.

**Figure 3.5 Save As dialog box**

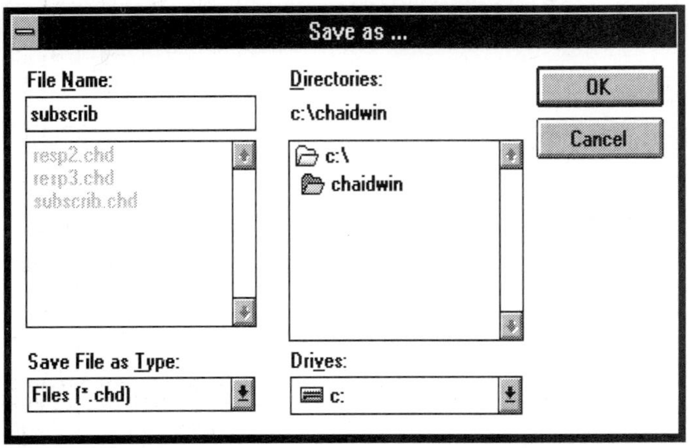


2. In the File Name box, type `resp2` to override the suggested filename and click on OK. This tells CHAID to save your analysis settings to an analysis file with the name *resp2.chd.* All printed and saved output will be prefixed by the name *resp2.*

As CHAID begins to scan the data file, progress is shown on a graduated line, along with the elapsed and remaining time. When scanning is complete, CHAID displays a report (including any error or informational messages) in the Scan Messages dialog box, as shown in Figure 3.6.

**Figure 3.6 Scan Messages dialog box**

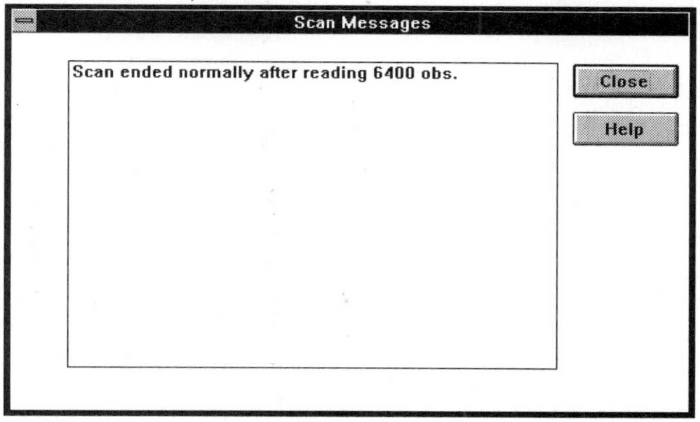


③ Click on Close. The Scan Results dialog box appears, as shown in Figure 3.7.

**Figure 3.7 Scan Results dialog box**

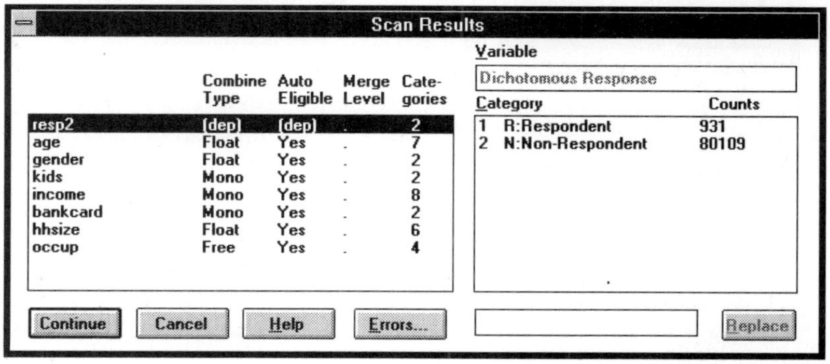


If you have defined everything correctly, your screen should appear as shown in Figure 3.7, above.

## Changing Symbols and Labels

You can change category symbols and labels for any variable within the Scan Results dialog box. We'll override the default symbols for *hhsize* that were derived from the SPSS system file value labels. The one-character symbols are used to identify categories in the tree diagram. Labels are displayed in before-merging crosstabulations.

To change the values for *hhsize*:

1. Click on *hhsize.*
2. Click on Category 5 in the Category box.
3. The label F: Five or more appears highlighted in the text box below the Category box, as shown in Figure 3.8. Change the label to 5:5 or more.
4. Click on Replace to replace the symbol and label.
5. Click on Continue to return to the Assign Variables dialog box.

**Figure 3.8 Scan Results dialog box with category 5 of hhsize selected**

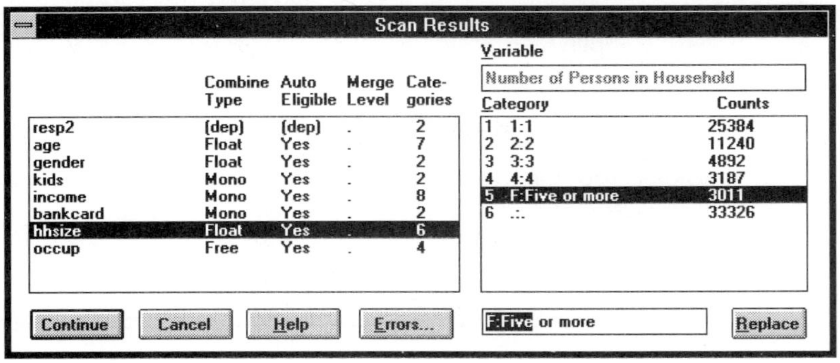

## Generating the Tree

To generate the tree diagram, click on OK. A series of messages tells you that the data are being analyzed. A horizontal bar shows how much of the data have been analyzed. When complete, your screen should resemble Figure 3.9.

**Figure 3.9 Tree Diagrams**

Global

Local

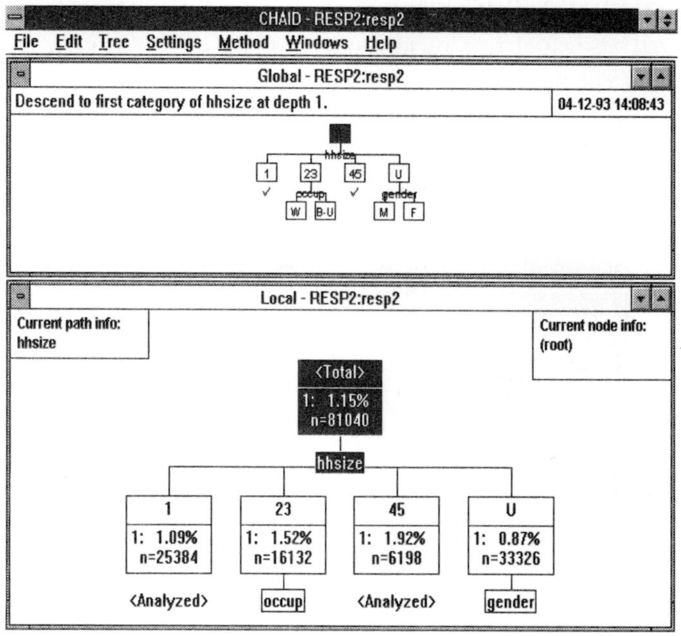


### Controlling the Tree Display

You can view a tree diagram in global and local modes. Except for very large trees, **global mode** shows the entire tree on your screen, as in the top half of Figure 3.9. **Local mode**, shown in the bottom half of Figure 3.9, gives you a close-up view of one parent node and up to five of its child nodes, so you get more detail about a section of the tree than global mode gives you. You may choose the contents of the nodes through the Windows menu.

## Crosstabulations

The Table window option displays a crosstabulation of the dependent variable (columns) by the current predictor variable (rows). You can control whether the table displays row percentages, column percentages, total percentages, or cell frequencies, and whether the table shows merged or unmerged categories of the predictor.

## After-Merge Table

To view a crosstabulation showing row percentages for merged categories of *hhsize*:

1. Highlight the root node on the tree diagram.
2. Double-click on the root node to display the After-Merge table, as shown in Figure 3.10. (You may need to resize this window, depending on the size of the table.)

Values in the Respondent column match the values displayed in each of the four *hhsize* nodes in Figure 3.10.

**Figure 3.10 After-Merge Table**

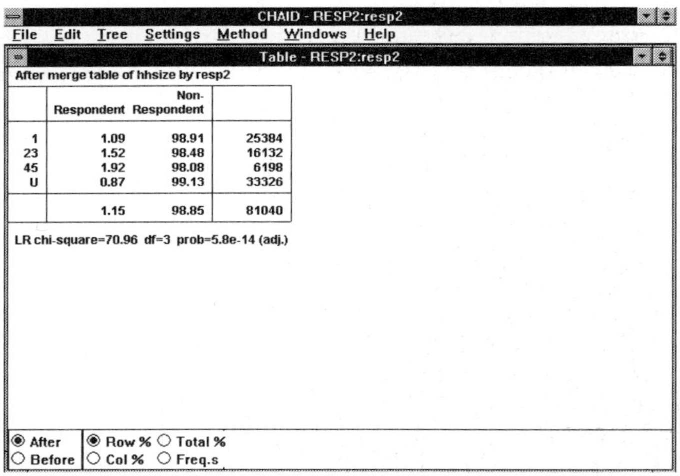


| | Respondent | Non-Respondent | |
|---|---|---|---|
| 1 | 1.09 | 98.91 | 25384 |
| 23 | 1.52 | 98.48 | 16132 |
| 45 | 1.92 | 98.08 | 6198 |
| U | 0.87 | 99.13 | 33326 |
| | 1.15 | 98.85 | 81040 |

Notice that CHAID merged categories 2 and 3, as well as categories 4 and 5.

The probability displayed in the bottom of the after-merge table, $5.8 \times 10^{-14}$, is adjusted for the fact that categories have been merged. The probability used by CHAID to rank predictors is the smaller of this adjusted probability and the probability associated with the table computed before category merging. (For information about how probabilities are computed, see Appendix B.)

## Before-Merge Table

To view a row percentage table of *hhsize* by *resp2* for unmerged *hhsize* categories:

- Click on Before in the bottom left corner of the Tables window. CHAID automatically produces a table of row percentages before *hhsize* categories are merged, as shown in Figure 3.11.

**Figure 3.11 Before-Merge Table**

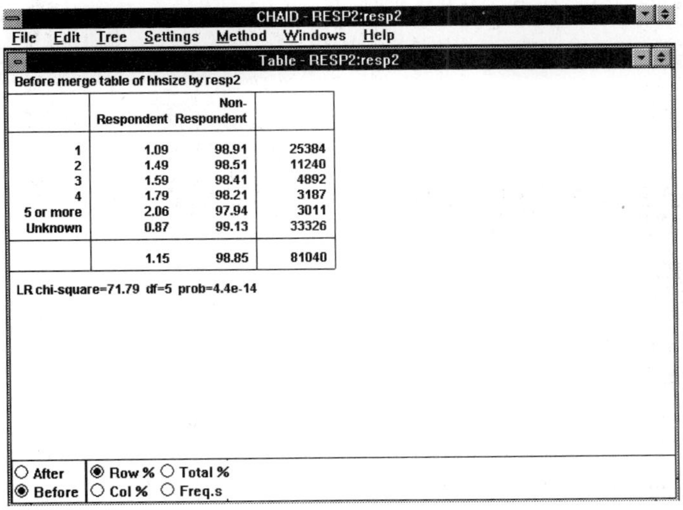


| | Respondent | Non-Respondent | |
|---|---|---|---|
| 1 | 1.09 | 98.91 | 25384 |
| 2 | 1.49 | 98.51 | 11240 |
| 3 | 1.59 | 98.41 | 4892 |
| 4 | 1.79 | 98.21 | 3187 |
| 5 or more | 2.06 | 97.94 | 3011 |
| Unknown | 0.87 | 99.13 | 33326 |
| | 1.15 | 98.85 | 81040 |

The table shows you the percentage of households in each *hhsize* category that responded to the promotion. For example, 1.09% of one-person households responded. Note that the total count in the lower right corner of the table (81,040) corresponds to the size of the highlighted node.

The table also displays the probability value ($p$ value), a measure of statistical significance. The smaller the $p$ value, the more statistically significant the predictor. The $p$ value for *hhsize* before categories are merged is $4.4e - 14$ (shorthand for $4.4 \times 10^{-14}$, a highly significant result). In fact, *hhsize* is the most significant of all the predictors. That is why the first split in the tree is based on household size categories.

## Comparing Crosstabulations Before and After Merging

To see why some of the categories of *hhsize* have been merged, compare the Before- and After-Merge tables (see Figure 3.11 and Figure 3.10). CHAID merged two-person and three-person households because their before-merge response rates (1.49% and 1.59%) are not significantly different. The combined response rate for the merged categories is 1.52%, as shown in Figure 3.10. Similarly, CHAID merges four- and five-person households, since the response rates for these subgroups (1.79% and 2.06%) are statistically indistinguishable. The combined response rate for the joint category is 1.92%.

## Obtaining Frequency Counts

To obtain frequency counts before *hhsize* categories are merged:

- Click on Freq.s in the Tables window. CHAID automatically produces the table of frequency counts shown in Figure 3.12.

**Figure 3.12 Table of frequency counts**

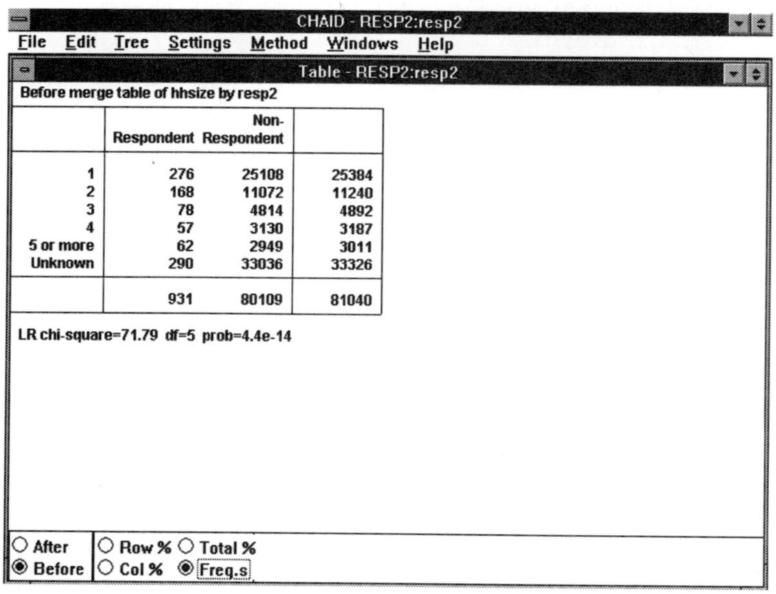


| | Respondent | Non-Respondent | |
|---|---|---|---|
| 1 | 276 | 25108 | 25384 |
| 2 | 168 | 11072 | 11240 |
| 3 | 78 | 4814 | 4892 |
| 4 | 57 | 3130 | 3187 |
| 5 or more | 62 | 2949 | 3011 |
| Unknown | 290 | 33036 | 33326 |
| | 931 | 80109 | 81040 |

The first row of the table indicates that 276 one-person households responded. The response rate displayed on the tree diagram (1.09%) is obtained by dividing the frequency by the total number of one-person households (25,384).

## Gains Charts

The results of a CHAID analysis can also be shown in the form of **gains charts**, which summarize tree segments in the form of a quantile array. For a dichotomous dependent variable, the default gains chart ranks segments on the percentage of cases in the first category of the dependent variable. Since the first category of *resp2* contains respondents, the default gains chart for the magazine subscription data ranks segments in terms of the proportion of households that responded to the mail promotion.

## Detailed Gains Charts

To produce a detailed gains chart for the magazine subscription data set:

1. Open the Windows menu and select Gains Chart Options.... This opens the Gains Chart Options dialog box, as shown in Figure 3.13.

**Figure 3.13 Gains Chart Options dialog box**

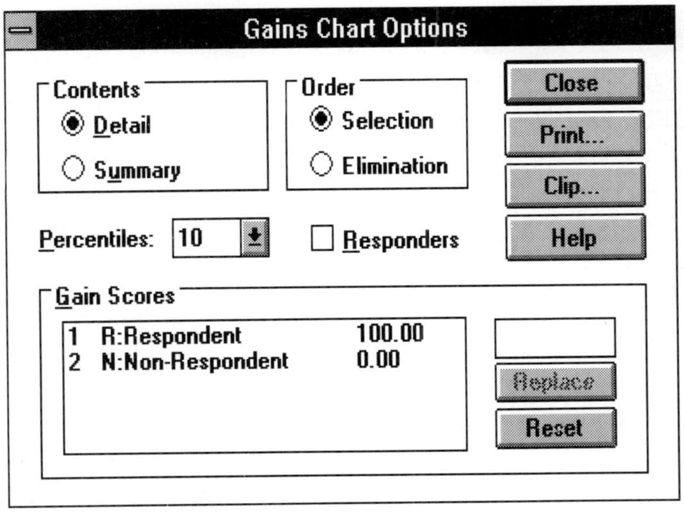


2. Click on Responders to add four columns to our detailed gains chart that contain the number of responders (*resp*) in each segment and the percentage of total responders (*%resp*) for each segment (for both individual and cumulative totals). This option is available only when one or more categories are singled out as the "response" categories and are each assigned a score of 100, while all other categories are assigned a score of 0.
3. Click on Close.
4. Open the Windows menu and select Gains Chart. CHAID displays a detailed gains chart, as shown in Figure 3.14. (Again, you may need to resize your window to see all of the chart.)

**Figure 3.14 Detailed gains chart**

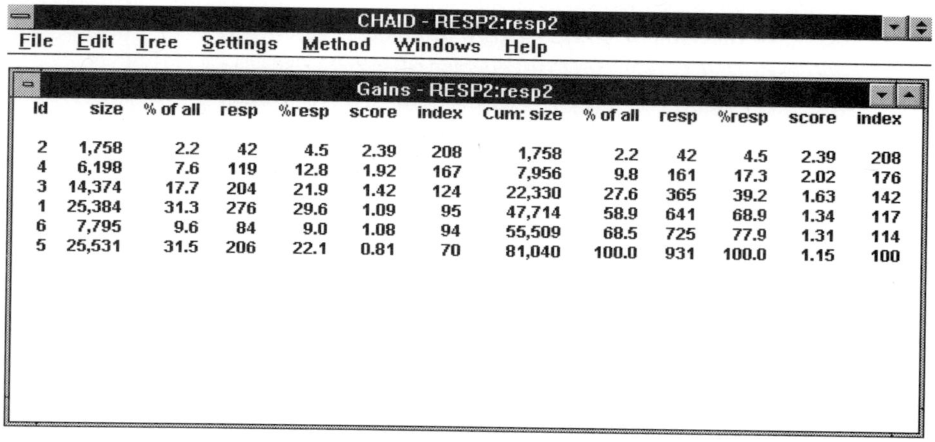


| Id | size | % of all | resp | %resp | score | index | Cum: size | % of all | resp | %resp | score | index |
|---|---|---|---|---|---|---|---|---|---|---|---|---|
| 2 | 1,758 | 2.2 | 42 | 4.5 | 2.39 | 208 | 1,758 | 2.2 | 42 | 4.5 | 2.39 | 208 |
| 4 | 6,198 | 7.6 | 119 | 12.8 | 1.92 | 167 | 7,956 | 9.8 | 161 | 17.3 | 2.02 | 176 |
| 3 | 14,374 | 17.7 | 204 | 21.9 | 1.42 | 124 | 22,330 | 27.6 | 365 | 39.2 | 1.63 | 142 |
| 1 | 25,384 | 31.3 | 276 | 29.6 | 1.09 | 95 | 47,714 | 58.9 | 641 | 68.9 | 1.34 | 117 |
| 6 | 7,795 | 9.6 | 84 | 9.0 | 1.08 | 94 | 55,509 | 68.5 | 725 | 77.9 | 1.31 | 114 |
| 5 | 25,531 | 31.5 | 206 | 22.1 | 0.81 | 70 | 81,040 | 100.0 | 931 | 100.0 | 1.15 | 100 |

In Figure 3.14, the column labeled *id* contains segment numbers. The score column displays the percentage of respondents in a segment. Thus, segment 2 had the highest response rate (2.39%). The index for a given segment measures the average response score for that segment relative to the average score for the total sample. The index score for segment 2 (208), which is computed as (2.39% / 1.15%) x 100, means that the response rate for this segment was 108% higher than average.

Columns 8 through 13 in the gains chart give you cumulative statistics. From the columns labeled *Cum: size*, *% of all*, and *score*, you can see that the three highest responding segments constitute 27.6% of the sample and have a combined response rate of 1.63%. The final column, *Cum: index*, measures the cumulative average response score for these segments relative to the average score for the total sample. For example, the index for the three best segments is 142 (1.63% / 1.15%). Thus, the three best segments, taken together, responded at a rate 42% higher than average.

## Segment Definitions

You can obtain segment definitions in the gains chart. For example, to obtain a segment definition for segment 3, double click on 3 in the *id* column in the gains chart. CHAID displays the variable names and group category that define this segment, as shown in the

Path dialog box in Figure 3.15. If you select Goto, CHAID will place you on the node that refers to this segment when you return to the tree diagram.

**Figure 3.15 Path dialog box**

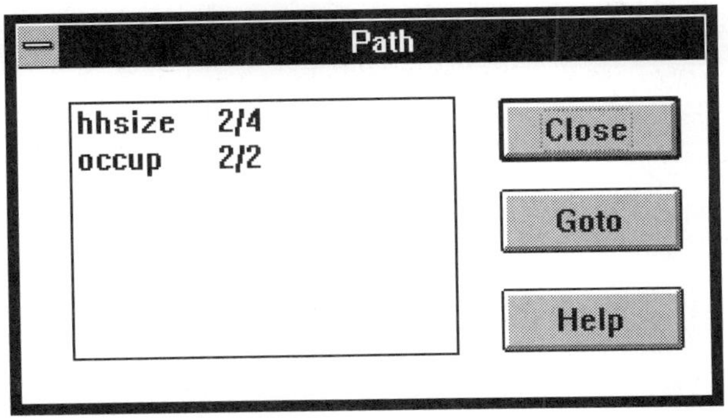


## Summary Gains Chart

A summary gains chart displays cumulative results at fixed percentage points of the cumulative segment size total. That is, a summary gains chart tells you the results that would have been obtained if the promotion had been mailed only to the highest-scoring segments.

We will illustrate the use of the summary gains chart as a dynamic research tool, where it plays a role similar to the incremental $R^2$ statistic in stepwise regression. As in stepwise regression (or stepwise inclusion), we begin with the baseline model, which specifies that no variable is predictive of *resp2*.

To obtain a summary gains chart:

1. Move to the root node of the tree diagram.
2. Open the Tree menu and select Prune. A warning will appear that the entire tree will be erased. Click on Continue to erase the tree.

   The root node shows that the overall response rate is 1.15% for the 81,040 households who were mailed. Under the baseline model, each household is predicted to respond at the same rate, 1.15%.
3. Open the Windows menu and select Gains Chart Options... to open the Gains Chart Options dialog box.
4. Under Contents, click on Summary, and then click on Responders if it has not already been selected.
5. Click on Close.

6. Open the Windows menu and select Gains Charts... (if it has not already been selected). This opens the Gains chart window with the summary chart, as shown in Figure 3.16. (You will need to resize your windows to have them look like Figure 3.16 through

**Figure 3.16 Gains summary chart**

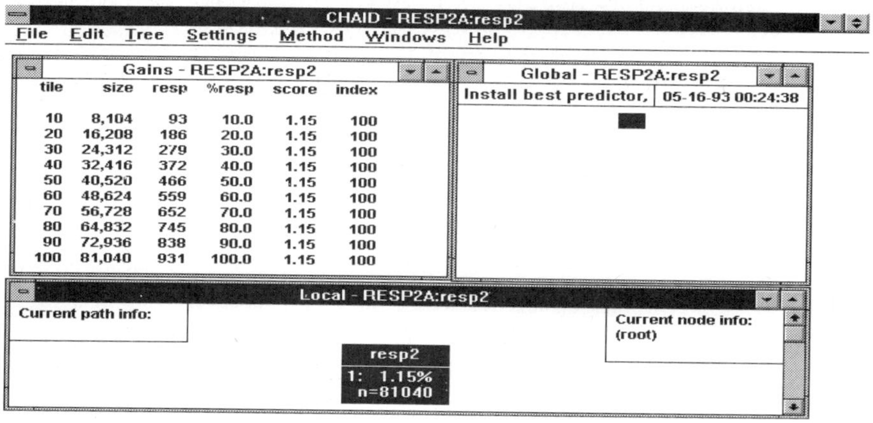


Figure 3.18. Resized in this way, you will be able to see the gains chart change automatically as you grow the tree.)

The summary gains chart summarizes the sample in ten rows representing cumulative deciles, where households are sorted from high to low with respect to the average score (that is, the response rate). Each decile contains exactly 1/10 of the sample, or 8104 households.

The gains chart summarizes the predicted response rate at various depths of the file. The *score* column shows that, under the baseline model, the predicted response rate is 1.15% regardless of whether 10%, 20%–90% or 100% of the file was mailed. From the bottom row, we see that the total number of responders is 1.15% of 81,040, or 931.

To update the gains chart with *hhsize* as the first predictor:

1. Open the Tree menu and click on Select... to open the Select Predictor dialog box.
2. Click on OK to select *hhsize* as the first predictor. Note that the 81,040 households are now divided into four subgroups based on the six categories of the *hhsize* variable.

The gains chart has been updated for this new variable and now shows that the best decile contains 148, or 15.9% of the 931 responders (see Figure 3.17). This decile is predicted to respond at 1.83%. This decile contains all 6,198 households known to have four or more people (response rate of 1.92%), plus a small number of the other households.

**Figure 3.17 Gains chart with hhsize as predictor**

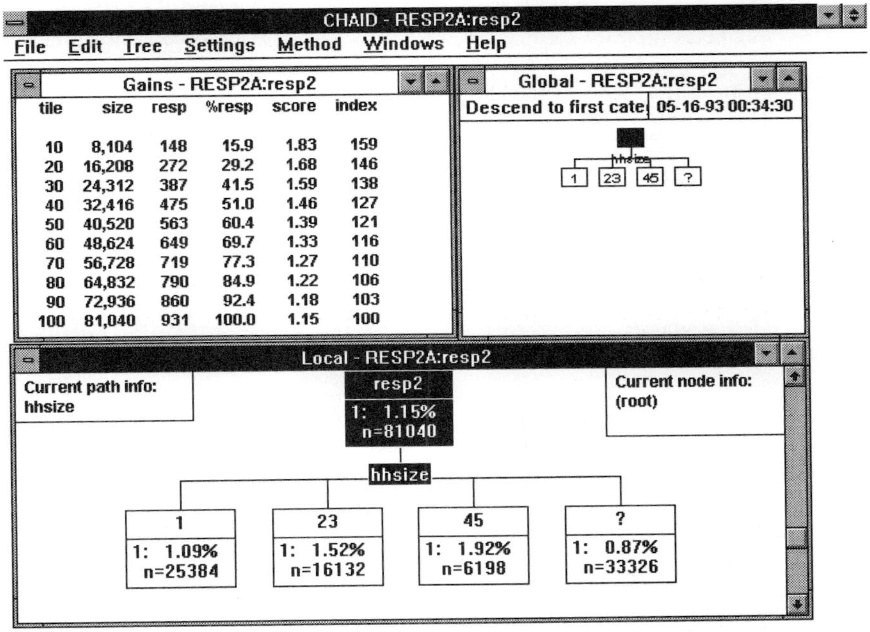


Next, segment the population again:

1. Using the mouse or arrow keys, move to the *hhsize* = 23 node.
2. Open the Tree menu and click on Select.... CHAID displays the Select Predictor dialog box.
3. Click on OK to select *occup* as the next predictor.
4. Highlight *occup* on the tree node.

In Figure 3.18 notice that the gains chart has been updated based on the two predictor variables.

The gains chart now summarizes the results in deciles based on ordering the sample according to the predicted response rates from the final segments. The predicted response rate for the best decile is now 2.01%. This decile contains all 1758 households known to have 2 to 3 people and a white collar occupation, plus all 6198 households known to

**Figure 3.18 Gains chart based on two predictor variables**

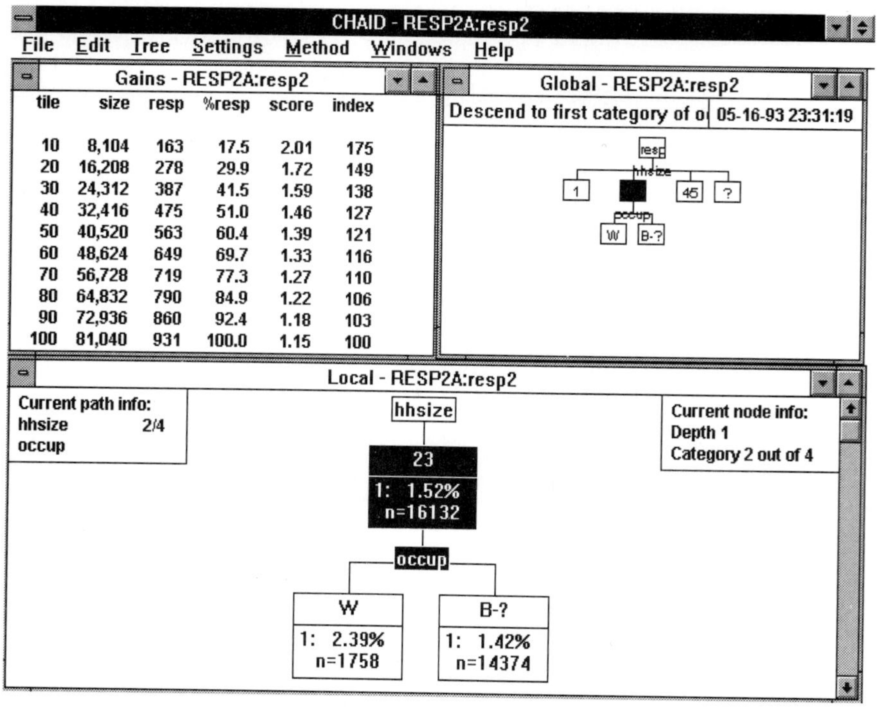

| tile | size | resp | %resp | score | index |
|---|---|---|---|---|---|
| 10 | 8,104 | 163 | 17.5 | 2.01 | 175 |
| 20 | 16,208 | 278 | 29.9 | 1.72 | 149 |
| 30 | 24,312 | 387 | 41.5 | 1.59 | 138 |
| 40 | 32,416 | 475 | 51.0 | 1.46 | 127 |
| 50 | 40,520 | 563 | 60.4 | 1.39 | 121 |
| 60 | 48,624 | 649 | 69.7 | 1.33 | 116 |
| 70 | 56,728 | 719 | 77.3 | 1.27 | 110 |
| 80 | 64,832 | 790 | 84.9 | 1.22 | 106 |
| 90 | 72,936 | 860 | 92.4 | 1.18 | 103 |
| 100 | 81,040 | 931 | 100.0 | 1.15 | 100 |



have four or more people (response rate of 1.92%), plus a small number of the other households.

With the Gains chart window open, you may also run an analysis in Automatic mode and watch the gains chart update automatically.

## Purpose of Gains Charts

If you know the **break-even response rate** (or if the category scores reflect profitability), you can use gains charts to determine the segments to which you should mail future promotions. For example, suppose that when you take into account the cost of mailing to nonresponders and unpaid responders, and the gain from paid responders, you need a response rate of 1.45% to break even. Looking at the Gains chart in Figure 3.18 (and assuming that this is your final segmentation), you would expect to make a profit if you mailed only to the top 40% of the households, since the score for these households (1.46%) exceeds the break-even level. Segments below this level were not profitable.

Alternatively, if the mail quantity was preset to 50,000, you could use the gains chart to pick the best 50,000 households to mail. Large savings could be gained by mailing only to segments with the highest response rates. For further information on the use of gains charts, see Derrick and Magidson (1992) and Magidson (1993b).

For information on how to use gains charts to rank segments based on the second category of a dichotomous dependent variable or based on a polytomous dependent variable, see "Gain Scores" on p. 122 in Chapter 6.

# 4 Getting Around in CHAID

The primary system functions of CHAID are listed on the menu bar of the Opening screen, as shown in Figure 4.1. This screen appears when you click on the CHAID icon.

**Figure 4.1 Opening screen**

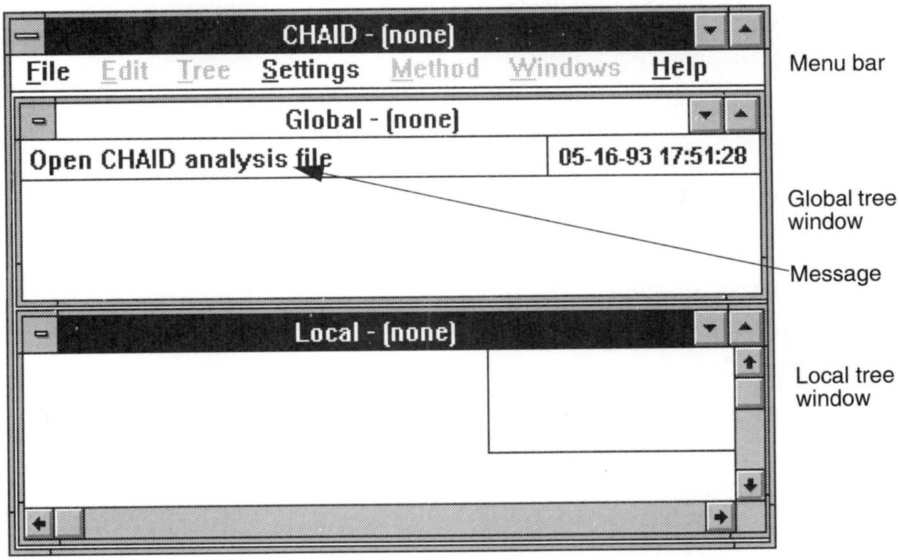


## Making Menu Selections

To open a menu, place the cursor on the menu bar. Use the arrow keys to move the cursor to the menu you want to open, or type in the highlighted letter of the name of the menu that you want to open. Then press ↵Enter or click on the name of the menu.

To make a selection from any menu, highlight the appropriate option by using the arrow keys and then pressing ↵Enter. Or, on an open menu, type the first highlighted letter in the option. For example, type O to use the Ordinal option on the Method menu. Remember the following rules when using the menus:

- Any option that has an ellipsis following it (for example, "Open...") will have further options for you to choose from.
- To exit from any menu, press Esc.
- Press any key to interrupt CHAID operations such as "Analyzing..." or "Recalling...."

# Moving Around on the Tree Diagram during an Analysis

Use the arrow keys to move from node to node on your tree diagram. The node that the cursor is in is called the **current node**, which is highlighted.

The caption at the top of the tree window shows the name of the current analysis and the dependent variable.

## Accelerator Keys

A series of accelerator keys can be used in place of menu selections for various CHAID specifications. To use the accelerator keys, press Ctrl and the accelerator key simultaneously while in the tree window. The operations performed by the accelerator keys are shown in Table 4.1.

**Table 4.1 Accelerator keys**

| Key | Operation |
|---|---|
| Ctrl - A | Tree Auto |
| Ctrl - C | Edit Copy |
| Ctrl - F | Tree Find Current Node |
| Ctrl - G | Windows Gains Chart |
| Ctrl - L | Tree Scroll Categories |
| Ctrl - N | File New |
| Ctrl - O | File Open |
| Ctrl - P | File Print |
| Ctrl - R | Tree Rearrange |
| Ctrl - S | Tree Select |
| Ctrl - T | Windows Table Window |
| Del | Tree Prune |
| ↵Enter | Tree Next |

# How to Obtain a Final Segmentation

CHAID gives you two ways to explore your data. In **automatic mode**, CHAID controls the entire analysis. In **interactive mode**, you control the analysis.

CHAID tells you the next step that it would perform if it were operating in automatic mode. This information, which is intended to guide you through your analysis, is available at any point in the analysis. (It is displayed on a message bar that appears on the upper left corner of the Global window.) You may elect whether or not to follow CHAID's suggestion. For example, in some cases you may want to split a node, using a predictor other than the one that CHAID selects. You can choose a different predictor immediately or after examining the results of splitting on a particular predictor.

## Interactive Mode

Let's analyze the magazine subscription data in interactive mode. First, you need to load the sample CHAID analysis file *resp2a.chd.*

To load the file:

1. Open the File menu, select Open, highlight *resp2a.chd*, and then click on OK.
2. Select Yes when CHAID asks you if you want to retrieve the previously saved tree.

The tree diagram appears on your screen, as shown in Figure 4.2.

**Figure 4.2 Tree diagram**

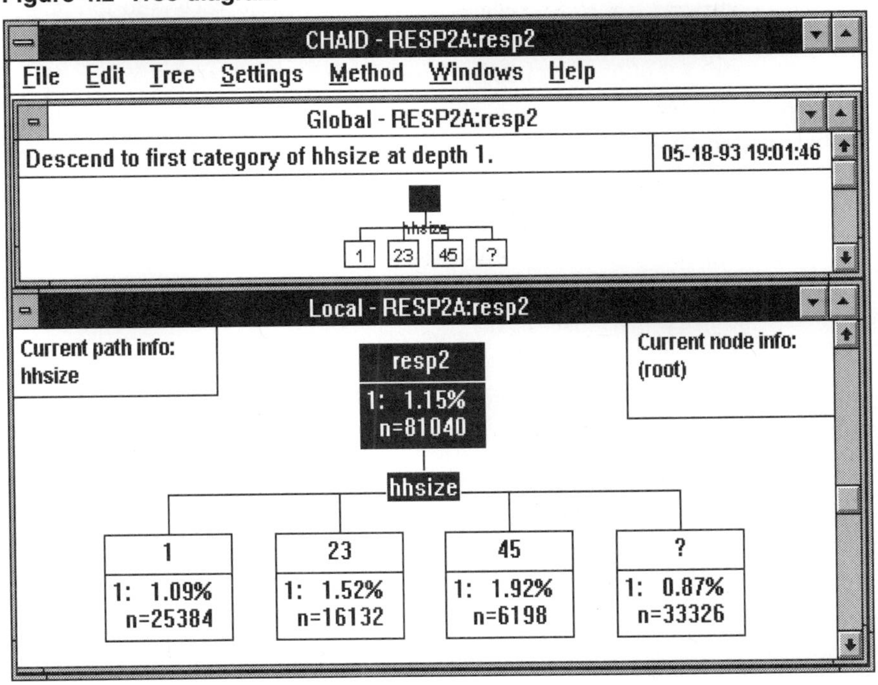

You can see that CHAID split only the root node. That's because when this analysis file was set up, the startup mode was specified as first-predictor mode instead of automatic mode. When first-predictor mode is selected, CHAID splits the root node on the first (best) predictor and then gives you control of any subsequent splits. (Startup mode is specified in standard options.)

The message bar tells you the next step that CHAID would carry out under automatic mode. This step depends on which node you are in. If you start in interactive mode and always follow the message bar's advice, you will build the same tree step by step just as CHAID would have built automatically.

Note that the root node on the tree diagram is highlighted and that the message bar says Descend to first category of hhsize at depth 1. This means that CHAID's next step would be to analyze and attempt to split the first category of *hhsize*.

To perform the next step suggested by CHAID on the message bar, you can either select Next on the Tree menu or simply press [↵Enter].

In the following steps, we will use the [↵Enter] key:

1. Press [↵Enter] to execute the next step. The cursor moves to the node for one-person households. On the message bar appears the message: Analyze subgroup and identify best predictor.

2. Press [↵Enter] to analyze the one-person subgroup.

CHAID begins analyzing the data set to find the most significant predictor to split the node containing one-person households. After CHAID displays Analyzing... and Please Wait messages, a selection box appears with the message: No significant predictors. This means that CHAID did not find any significant predictors to split this subgroup on.

3. Press [↵Enter] to return to the tree diagram. The message bar now displays Move to category # 2 of hhsize at depth 1 (no predictor available).

4. Press [↵Enter] to execute the next step. The cursor moves to the node for two- and three-person households. Again, the message Analyze subgroup and identify best predictor appears.

5. Press [↵Enter]. CHAID computes probability values for each predictor and displays a list of significant predictors ranked in order of their probabilities, as shown in Figure 4.3. The predictor with the lowest probability (*occup*) is shown at the top of the list.

**Figure 4.3 List of significant predictors**

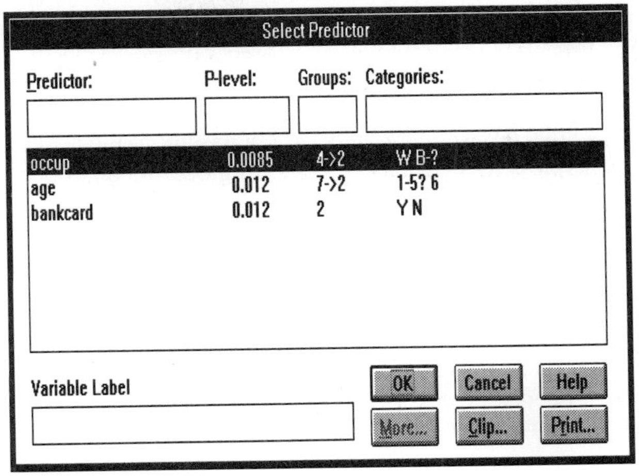


❻ Press ↵Enter to select *occup*. The node containing two- and three-person households is split according to the merged categories of *occup*. CHAID allows you to split on any variable on the predictors list. To select one of the others, you would use the arrow keys to highlight the variable and then press ↵Enter.

❼ Continue pressing ↵Enter or selecting Next until you get a good feel for how CHAID takes you through an analysis.

## Automatic Mode

At any point in the analysis, you can allow CHAID to assume control of the analysis. Select Auto from the Tree menu (or specify Automatic as the Startup mode in standard options). CHAID automatically expands the tree below the current node until there are no more significant predictors, or until user-defined limitations are met. Automatic mode will build on any existing splits but will not overwrite them.

When CHAID decides not to split a node, the message bar tells you why. For example, at depth limit or segment too small might appear at the end of your message. This means that you have reached a preset stopping level. To override these levels, you can use the Select option (see “Selecting Predictors” on p. 38). Other messages you may see include No Significant Predictors or No Predictors with >2 categories.

To automatically expand the tree, follow these steps:

❶ Highlight the root node of the tree diagram.

❷ Open the Tree menu and select Auto.

CHAID displays a series of Analyzing... messages until it has finished expanding the tree. Press any key to interrupt the analysis.

When CHAID completes an automatic analysis, it returns control to you. You can then examine and print a copy of the results (using the Print option on the File menu) or modify the resulting segmentation (see "How to Modify the Tree," below).

For any subgroup that CHAID has analyzed but has not found a significant predictor in, Analyzed appears directly beneath the node. In global mode, a check mark (✓) appears below the node. Analyzed does not appear beneath nodes that were not split due to user-defined settings.

# How to Modify the Tree

CHAID gives you three ways to modify a tree: pruning splits, selecting different predictor variables, and changing the ways in which predictor categories are merged (rearranging categories).

## Pruning Splits

You may decide that certain splits, though statistically significant, are not substantively significant—that is, the split shows only modest differences between categories of the selected predictor. You can make your tree more parsimonious by deleting a split (whenever a split is deleted, all the splits below it are also deleted). To remove unwanted splits, use the Prune option.

To prune all splits in our example:

1. Highlight the root node of the tree diagram.
2. Open the Tree menu and select Prune. CHAID warns you that the entire tree below the selected node will be erased.
3. Select Yes. Only the root node remains on your screen.

## Selecting Predictors

Another way to modify the tree is to select a different predictor to split a subgroup. Suppose that you want to change the predictor that was originally selected as the best split. For example, you may want to see what the tree would look like if you initially split on *income* instead of *hhsize*.

To select a new predictor, open the Tree menu and choose Select. CHAID recalls the data and displays a list of predictors, as shown in Figure 4.4. Notice that *income* does not appear on the list of predictors. By default, CHAID lists only predictors that are statistically significant.

**Figure 4.4 List of significant predictors**

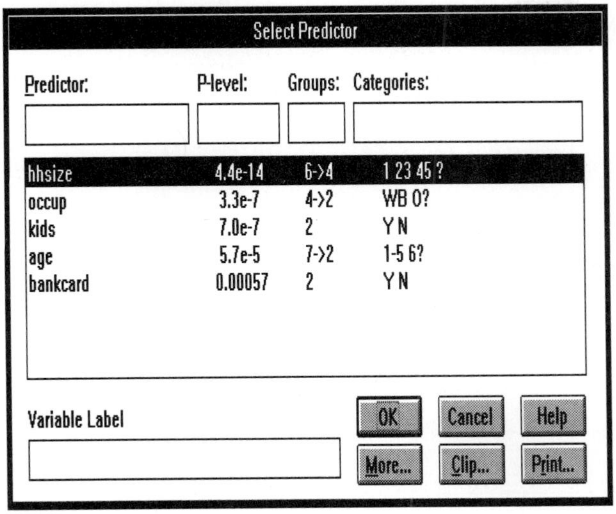


Optionally, you can list all predictors or only those that are at least marginally significant (that is, predictors for which not all categories have been merged).

To get the full list of predictors:

❶ Click on More... to display a list of options for controlling how predictors are displayed, as shown in Figure 4.5.

**Figure 4.5 Predictor Display Options dialog box**

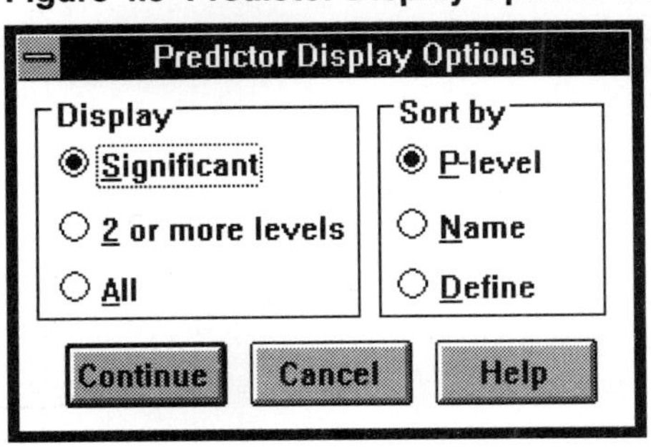

2. Click on All in the Display box and then click on Continue. CHAID displays the full list of predictors, as shown in Figure 4.6.

**Figure 4.6 Full list of predictors**

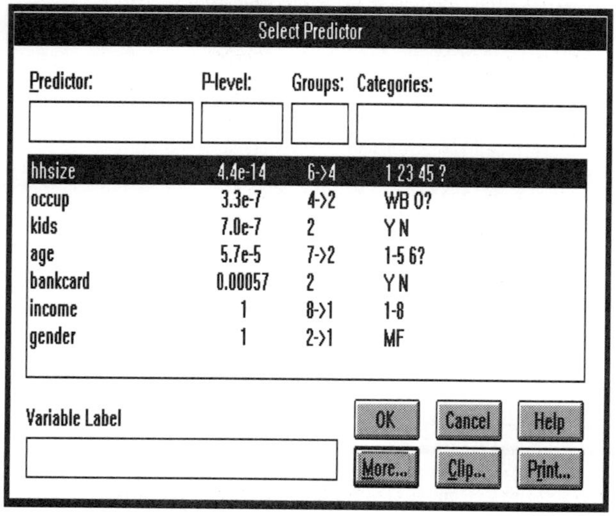


3. Select *income* to be the predictor by highlighting *income* and clicking on OK.

   CHAID inserts *income* as the first split on your tree. You can see that all original eight categories of *income* were merged into one category, so this is not really a helpful split. We will deal with that in the next section.

## Using Tables When Selecting a New Split

To see why CHAID has merged all categories of *income*, let's examine the crosstabulation for *income* by *resp2* before *income* categories are merged.

1. Highlight the root node.
2. Double-click the root node to bring up the Tables window.
3. Click on Before. CHAID displays all income categories before they were merged, as shown in Figure 4.7.

**Figure 4.7 Table of response rate by income**

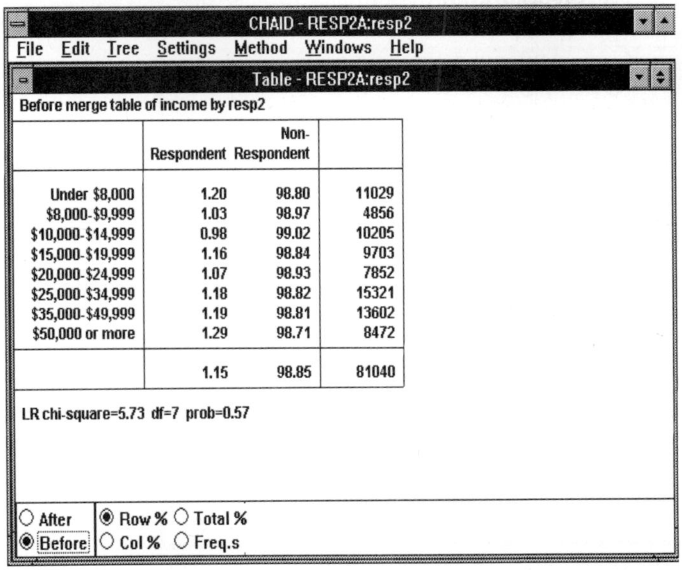


| | Respondent | Non-Respondent | |
|---|---|---|---|
| Under $8,000 | 1.20 | 98.80 | 11029 |
| $8,000-$9,999 | 1.03 | 98.97 | 4856 |
| $10,000-$14,999 | 0.98 | 99.02 | 10205 |
| $15,000-$19,999 | 1.16 | 98.84 | 9703 |
| $20,000-$24,999 | 1.07 | 98.93 | 7852 |
| $25,000-$34,999 | 1.18 | 98.82 | 15321 |
| $35,000-$49,999 | 1.19 | 98.81 | 13602 |
| $50,000 or more | 1.29 | 98.71 | 8472 |
| | 1.15 | 98.85 | 81040 |

You can see that all eight categories of *income* responded at about the same rate. While some categories differ from the overall rate (1.15%), the differences are not statistically significant.

4. Return to the tree diagram by reducing the Tables window with the down arrow.

## Changing How Predictor Categories Are Merged

You can merge the categories of a predictor in any manner allowed by the predictor combine-type setting whether or not the merge is statistically significant. After you change the way the categories are merged, CHAID displays the probability associated with the rearranged predictor. For example, suppose you want to compare response rates for lower incomes (less than $50,000) and higher incomes ($50,000 or more). To do this, you need to group the eight categories of income into two new categories: 1 through 7 for lower income and 8 for higher income.

To manually rearrange the categories of *income*:

1. Highlight the root node of the tree diagram.
2. Open the Tree menu and select Rearrange. All eight categories of *income* are displayed, as shown in Figure 4.8.

**Figure 4.8 Rearrange Categories dialog box**

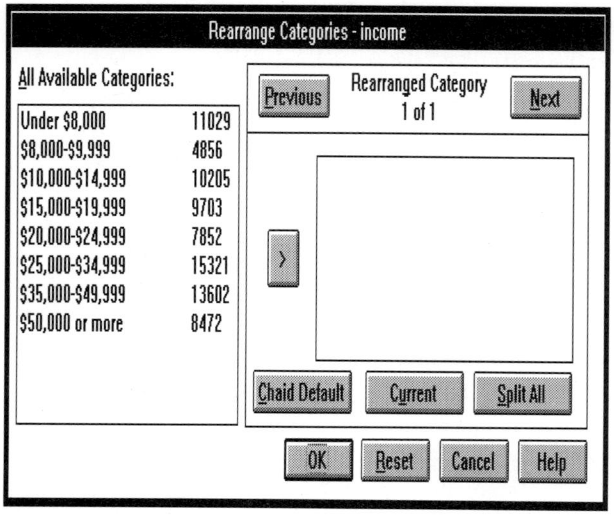


3. Click and drag to highlight the first seven categories.
4. Click on the right arrow button. The categories appear in the box to the right labeled Rearranged Category 1 of 1.
5. Click on Next.
6. Highlight the last category and click on the right arrow button.
7. Click on OK.

As shown in Figure 4.9, CHAID merges the original eight *income* categories into two (1 through 7 on the left and 8 on the right).

**Figure 4.9 Tree for new income categories**

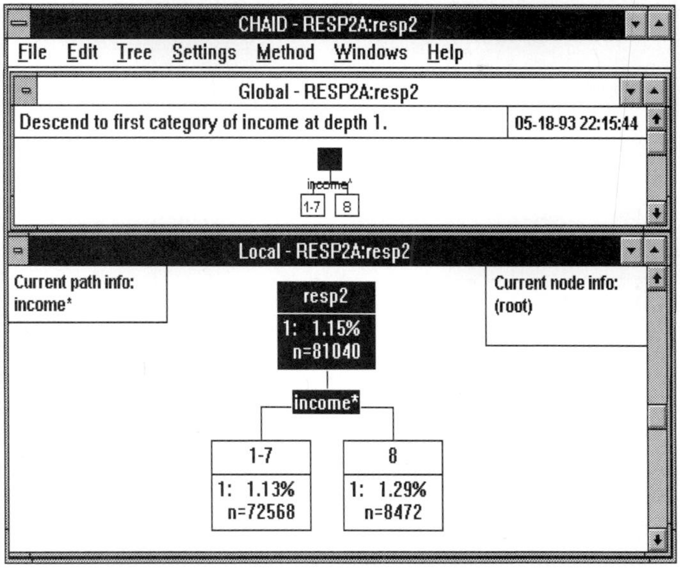


## Rearranging Categories

CHAID offers tables and statistics to help you judge the goodness of any split you specify and to compare these segmentations with the split that CHAID suggests.

To display the statistical significance of your new arrangement of *income* categories, follow these steps:

1. Highlight the root node of the tree diagram. Double-click to bring up the Tables window.
2. Click on After.

This gives you a table of *income** by *resp2*, as shown in Figure 4.10, after the *income* categories are merged. CHAID uses the asterisk (*) to remind you that *income* has been rearranged. Since the probability value, listed at the bottom of the table, is 0.82, chi-square is not statistically significant at the 0.05 level. Remember, if you can't see all of the table, you may need to resize the window.

**Figure 4.10 Table of response rate for new income**

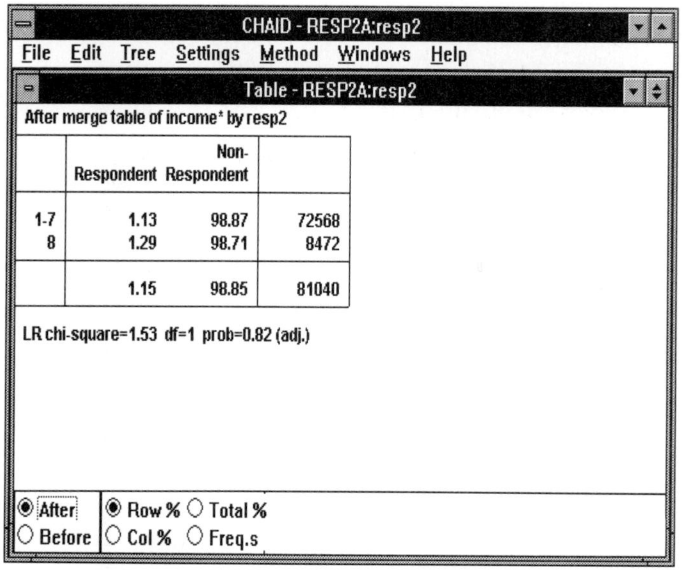


## Reverting to the Original Categories

To revert to the original category grouping:

1. Highlight the root node.
2. Open the Tree menu and select Rearrange.
3. Click on CHAID Default.
4. Click on OK.

CHAID reverts to its original merging of all eight categories. Since this split is not very useful, select *hhsize* as the current predictor:

1. Press Ctrl-S to display the list of predictors.
2. Click on OK to select *hhsize*.

## Obtaining Details of Predictor Categories

Predictor categories are identified by a one-character symbol and a detailed label. The nodes show only the category symbols.

To view the detailed category labels:

1. Highlight the root node.
2. Open the Settings menu and select Variable Categories. CHAID displays detailed labels for the categories of *hhsize*, as shown in Figure 4.11.

**Figure 4.11 Variable Categories dialog box**

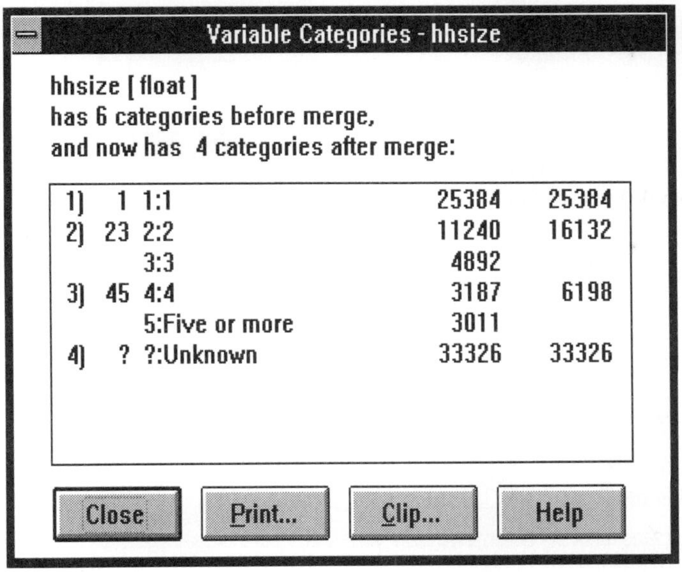


A message tells you that CHAID has merged the original six categories into four. CHAID also tells you which of the original categories belongs in each of the new categories after merging and provides counts for categories both before and after merging.

3. Click on Close to return to the tree window.

## Getting Information about a Node

You can get information about the current node from the current path information box or from the current node information box located in the left and right corners of the local window.

### Current Node

Except when you are on the root node, a box in the upper right corner of the local window gives you information regarding the current node. The box shows the depth of the tree and the current category number for the current node. To see information for a different node, use the arrow keys to highlight the node.

### Current Path

In the upper left corner of the Local window, CHAID lists the predictors used to split at each level of the tree through the level of the current node and the current category.

The last line specifies what is at the next level of the tree. If nothing is specified, this tells you that you haven't yet attempted to split the current node for one-person households. If the subgroup were split, the name of the predictor would be displayed.

**Figure 4.12 Information for one-person households**

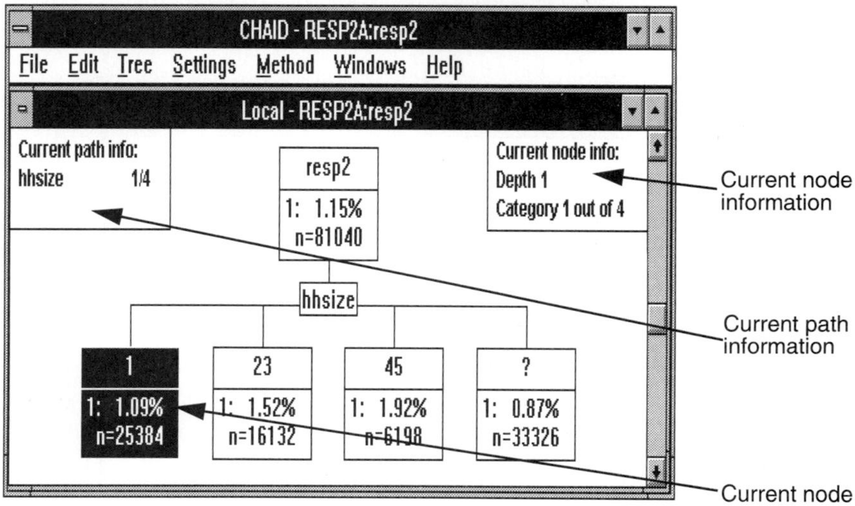


## Exiting from CHAID

To exit from CHAID:

1. Open the File menu, and then select Exit.

   CHAID displays this prompt, Exit Chaid?

2. Select Yes.

# 5 Using Category Scores

Scores assigned to the categories of a dependent variable can serve several purposes in CHAID:

- Category scores for an ordinal dependent variable provide a way to account for differential costs or gains associated with the categories. For example, in this chapter, we'll use category scores to weigh the relative gains associated with paid responders, unpaid responders, and nonresponders in a direct marketing promotion.
- Scores can be used to merge or omit categories of the dependent variable.
- Scores are used for gains charts produced in a CHAID analysis. You can produce gains charts based on different sets of category scores.
- Scores may be used to contrast or increase the distance between two categories while deleting others.

## Assigning Scores to Variables

When using scores, remember the following rules:

- If you treat the dependent variable as ordinal, you must assign scores to all categories of the dependent variable (you can tell CHAID to estimate any unknown scores). If an ordinal dependent variable is polytomous, these scores are used to assess statistical significance. By default, the average score of the dependent variable is displayed on the tree diagram. (Optionally, you can display the percentage distribution instead of the average score.)
- By altering the scores for an ordinal dependent variable, the segmentation criterion is changed and the resulting segmentation may be different. If you are not sure which scores to use, you can perform separate analyses using different scores and compare the resulting segmentations.
- Scores assigned to the categories of a dichotomous dependent variable are not used in the assessment of statistical significance. However, the average scores can be displayed on the tree diagram.
- If you treat the dependent variable as nominal, you do not need to assign category scores. Scores assigned to a nominal dependent variable do not affect the assessment of statistical significance.

## Assigning Scores to an Ordinal Dependent Variable

By default, if an ordinal dependent variable is numeric, the variable codes are used as category scores. If the variable contains string (non-numeric) codes for its categories, by default, CHAID orders the categories alphabetically and uses consecutive integers (for example, 1, 2, and 3) as category scores. In this case, you must be sure that the scores order the categories correctly.

For example, suppose that the categories of the string variable *severity* are "L" for "light," "M" for "moderate," and "E" for "extreme." Suppose further that the primary goal of the CHAID analysis is to contrast segments prone to extreme severity with those prone to light severity. The moderate category is assumed to be somewhere between the other categories on the severity dimension. By default, CHAID assigns the integer scores 1, 2, and 3 to E, L, and M. This means that the highest average score (3) is assigned to the middle category, which is incorrect.

You can modify the default scores prior to the analysis by selecting Edit Scores as the Startup mode. (See "Startup Mode" on p. 103 for more details.) If the analysis has already begun, you can open the Method menu and then select either Ordinal or Nominal to start a new analysis with different scores. You can provide your scores for the categories or tell CHAID to estimate the scores.

CHAID gives you the ability to specify analyses based on different scores. You can perform an analysis based on one set of scores (or use the nominal method that does not take category scores into account) and then modify the scores for a second analysis.

# How to Assign Category Scores

This example shows how to incorporate category scores into an analysis of a polytomous dependent variable. We will use the magazine subscription data set, but our dependent variable is *resp3*, coded 1 (paid responder), 2 (unpaid responder), and 3 (nonresponder). We'll compare a default nominal CHAID segmentation of *resp3* to an ordinal CHAID analysis that takes into account the gain (or loss) associated with each category of the dependent variable. For simplicity, we will limit the size of the trees by setting the depth limit to 2. This tutorial also shows how to use category scores to merge and delete categories of a dependent variable.

## Nominal Method

Although the segmentation under the nominal method is the same with or without scores, you can enter scores to display them on the tree diagram.

To assign scores and conduct the nominal analysis of *resp3*:

1. Open the CHAID analysis file *resp3.chd*. Select Yes when asked whether to retrieve the previously saved tree. When the tree appears, the root node is highlighted.
2. Open the Method menu and select Nominal even though Nominal is the default and is the current selection (indicated by a check mark next to it). The Edit Scores box will appear. Selection of Nominal or Ordinal from the Method menu is the only way in which you can assign new scores to dependent variable categories.
3. The first category (paid responders) is highlighted. To change a category's score, double-click on the category and then type in the new value.
4. Double-click on category 1 and then type 35 and click the mouse. This value represents the dollar amount gained when someone pays for a subscription.
5. Highlight the second category (unpaid responders). Double-click and enter –7. This value represents the cost of sending a sample copy and several more mailings to unpaid responders. Click the mouse.
6. Highlight the third category (nonresponders). Double-click and enter –.15. This value represents the $0.15 cost of a mailing that garners no response.
7. Click on OK. CHAID warns you that your present tree will be erased.
8. Click on Yes to continue. CHAID displays the Score Order dialog box.
9. Click on OK to keep the scores unordered. CHAID recalls the data and displays the root node.
10. Open the Tree menu and select Auto to run an automatic analysis. When CHAID completes the analysis, a tree diagram is displayed (see Figure 5.1).

Each node shows the percentage of cases that were paid responders, unpaid responders, or nonresponders.

**Figure 5.1 Tree diagram for resp3 showing percentages**

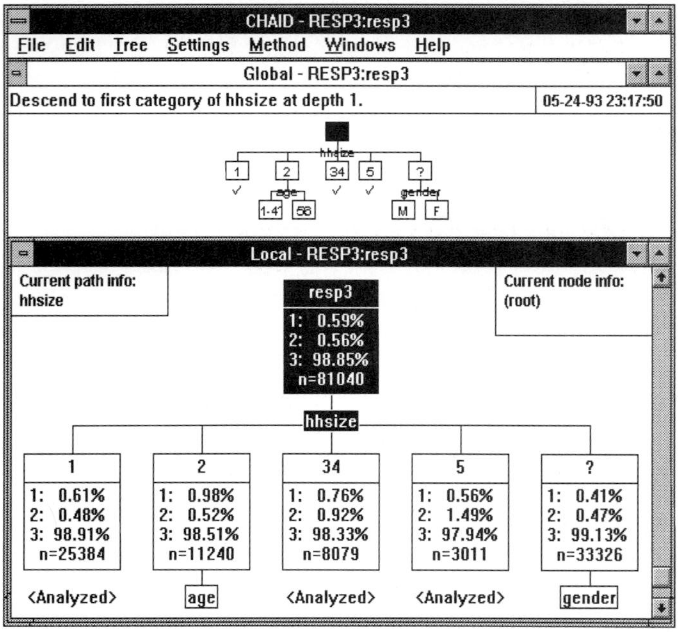


The tree diagram for *resp3* differs from our earlier analysis of *resp2* (see Chapter 2). While *hhsize* is still used for the first split, it is now merged into five categories instead of four. In our earlier analysis, *hhsize* categories 2 and 3 were merged. Now category 2 is a separate category and categories 3 and 4 are merged.

## Displaying Average Scores

It is difficult to determine which segments are the "best" from the tree displayed in Figure 5.1, since you have to weigh the percentage of paid responders against the percentage of unpaid responders and nonresponders. You can simplify the comparison of segments if you display average scores instead of percentages.

To display the average scores for each segment:

- Open the Windows menu and select Scores. The tree now displays a diagram of the average category scores for each segment, as shown in Figure 5.2.

**Figure 5.2 Tree diagram for resp3 showing average scores**

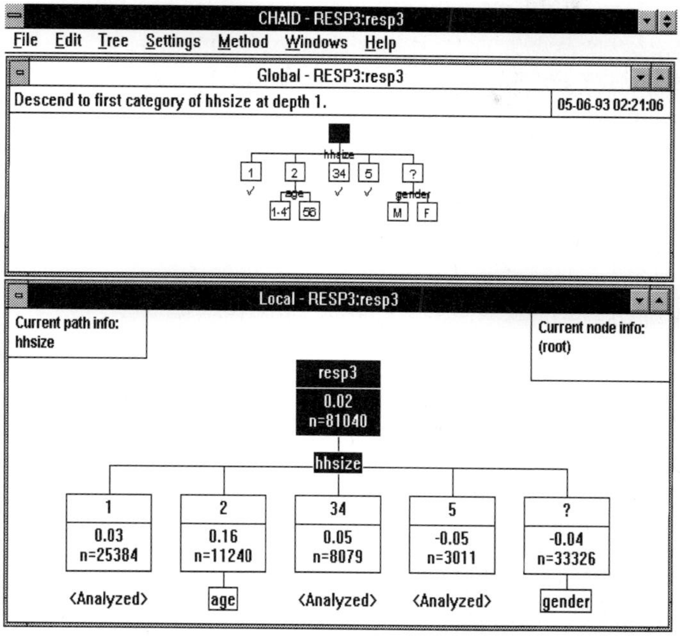


The score for a node is the expected gain associated with sending the promotional materials to a household in that subgroup. For example, the root node now contains 0.02, representing an average of $0.02 gained for each household in the sample. You can also see that an average of $0.16 was gained for each two-person household and $0.05 was lost for each household with five or more persons.

## Ordinal Method

Let's reanalyze *resp3* using the same category scores but treating the dependent variable as ordinal.

1. Open the Method menu and select Ordinal. The Edit Scores dialog box appears.
2. To keep the same scores that you have already entered, click on OK. CHAID warns you that your tree will be erased.
3. Click on Yes to continue.
4. Click on OK to keep the scores unordered. Only the root node appears on your screen.
5. Open the Tree menu and select Auto to run an automatic analysis.

When CHAID completes the analysis, a tree diagram is displayed, as shown in Figure 5.3.

**Figure 5.3 Tree diagram for resp3 using the ordinal method**

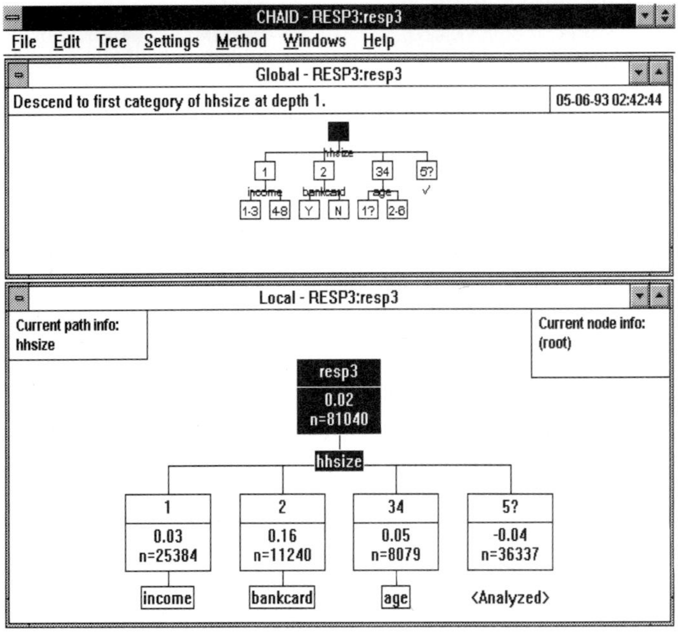


Note the following differences from the nominal analysis. First, while *hhsize* is still the most significant predictor, the categories of *hhsize* are merged into four subgroups instead of five. In particular, CHAID has merged households containing five persons and households containing an unknown number of individuals. These groups have been merged because they have similar average scores (–0.05 and –0.04), as shown in Figure 5.2.

At the next level in the tree, you again see results different from those provided by the nominal analysis. While the earlier analysis suggested that one-person households are a homogeneous segment with an expected gain of 0.03 per household (see Figure 5.2), the ordinal analysis divides one-person households based on income. Also, two-person households are split based on whether they own a bankcard, and three- and four-person households are split based on age.

To see the next level of the tree, click on *Income* on the local tree diagram. The split on one-person households is displayed, as shown in Figure 5.4.

**Figure 5.4 Split on one-person households**

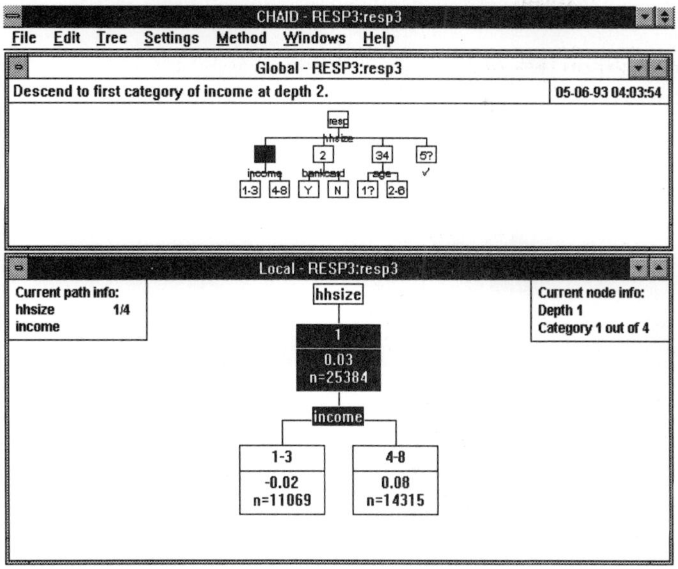


The variable *income* in the magazine subscription data set is an ordinal variable with eight categories (the lowest category is coded 1 and the highest category is coded 8). CHAID has divided one-person households into a low-income group (income categories 1 through 3) and a high-income group (categories 4 through 8). The tree shows that mailings to one-person households with high incomes result in an average gain of $0.08, while mailings to one-person households with low incomes result in an average loss of $0.02.

To see the split on two-person households, click on *hhsize* in the Local window, followed by *bankcard.* The split is displayed, as shown in Figure 5.5.

**Figure 5.5 Split on two-person households**

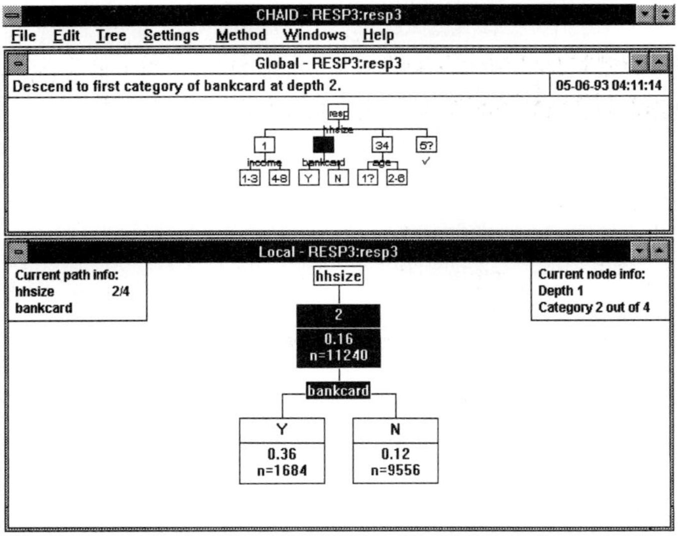


The expected gain for two-person households that own a bankcard (0.36) is three times greater than the expected gain for two-person households that do not own a bankcard (0.12).

To display the split on three- and four-person households (Figure 5.6), click on *hhsize* in the Local window, followed by *age.*

**Figure 5.6 Split on three- and four-person households**

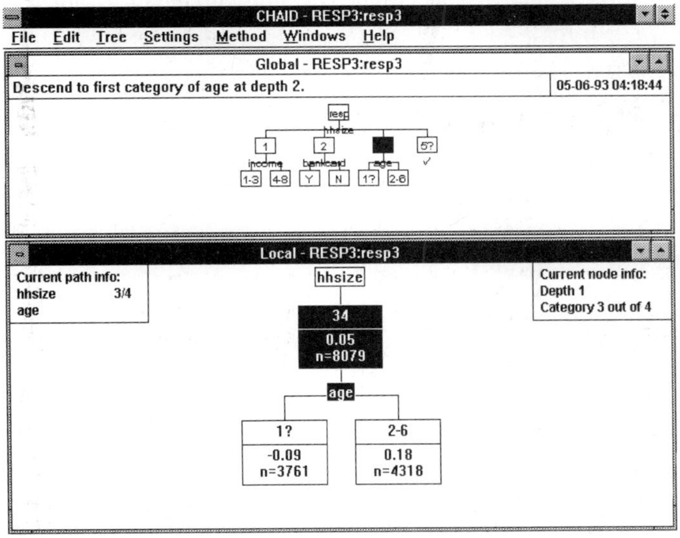


A loss of $0.09 per household is expected for three- and four-person households in which the age of the head of household is under 25 (coded 1) or unknown (coded ?). The node containing three- and four-person households of all other ages has the second highest average score (0.18).

Overall, the tree diagram suggests that the best segments for future magazine subscription promotions will tend to be two-person households and households with three or four persons in which the head of the household is older than 24. Segments having the lowest value are those containing households of unknown size and three- and four-person households in which the head of the household is under 25 or whose age is unknown.

## Merging Categories of the Dependent Variable

You can collapse the trichotomous variable *resp3* into a dichotomous variable that compares responders (paid and unpaid) to nonresponders by assigning the same score, 100, to each responder category and 0 to the nonresponder category. The analysis based on these scores will be equivalent to our analysis of the dichotomous variable *resp2* in Chapter 2.

To run the analysis where paid and unpaid responders are merged:

1. Open the Method menu and select Nominal to bring up the Edit Scores dialog box.
2. Enter a score of 100 for the first and second categories (paid responders and unpaid responders) and 0 for the last category (nonresponders).
3. Click on OK and then click on Yes to continue. The root node is displayed.
4. Open the Tree menu and select Auto to build the tree automatically. Notice that the tree diagram is identical to the first tree you built. (See Chapter 3.)

## Deleting Categories of the Dependent Variable

Now let's compare only paid and unpaid responders, ignoring nonresponders. You can delete nonresponders from the analysis by assigning a period (.) to the third category as its score.

To run an analysis without nonresponders:

1. Open the Method menu and select Ordinal to bring up the Edit Scores dialog box.

   On the category score list that appears, the first two categories of the dependent variable have been merged from our previous example.
2. Click on Reset to restore the original scores.
3. Enter a score of 100 for the first category (paid responders). Then enter 0 for the second category (unpaid responders) and a period (.) for the third category (nonresponders).
4. Click on OK and then click on Yes to continue.

The root node is displayed. The total number of respondents has dropped from 81,040 to 931 because nonresponders have been omitted from this analysis. Since we have reduced the size of our sample, we also need to change the stopping rules.

## Changing Stopping Rules

CHAID continues the splitting process for each subgroup until one of the following stopping rules is met:

- No more statistically significant splits are found.
- The sample size for the subgroup falls below the cutoff level for subgroup size.
- The depth level of the subgroup equals the limit on the number of splits CHAID is allowed to make in an automatic run.

To review the settings for the current analysis, open the Settings menu and select Options. The Standard Options dialog box appears, as shown in Figure 5.7.

**Figure 5.7 Standard Options dialog box**

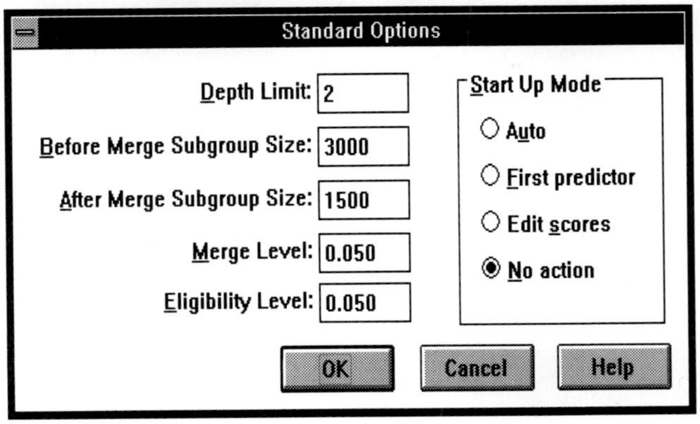


The maximum depth setting, 2, terminates the splitting of any parent group at level 2. The segment size settings were 1500 for After Merge Subgroup Size and 3000 for Before Merge Subgroup Size. The first setting means that no final segment can contain fewer than 1500 observations. The second setting prevents the splitting of any parent group containing fewer than 3000 observations. CHAID would not make any splits if we used the current settings, which are larger than the total sample.

To change the subgroup size settings:

1. Select Before Merge Subgroup Size and enter 100 in the text box.
2. Select After Merge Subgroup Size and enter 50 in the text box.
3. Click on OK.
4. Open the Tree menu and select Select.
5. When CHAID displays the Select Predictor dialog box, highlight *age* and click on OK.

The root node is now split by *age*, as shown in Figure 5.8.

**Figure 5.8 Tree diagram split on age**

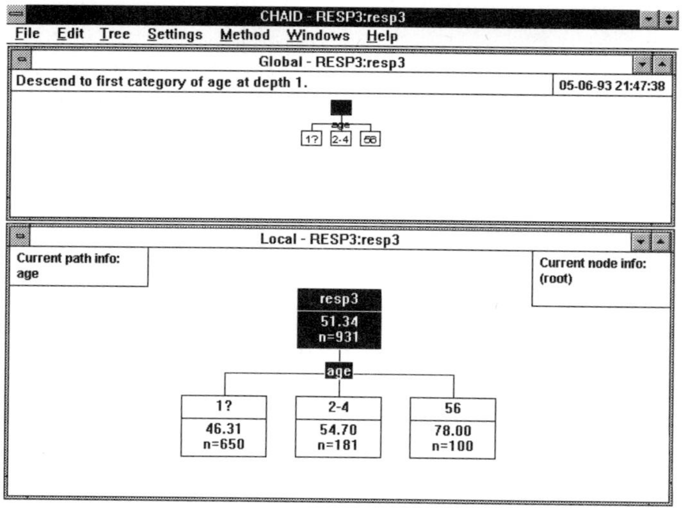


The average score displayed on the tree diagram is the percentage of responders who paid for a subscription. Responders living in households in which the head of the household is 55 or older are most likely to pay for their subscription. Remember that a CHAID segmentation of a dependent variable containing only two categories is identical whether it is performed using the nominal or ordinal method. (You can change to the nominal method and rerun the analysis to verify that the results are the same.)

# How to Calibrate Category Scores

Calibration has many applications in survey analysis, where Likert scales (in which sequential integers are assigned as category scores) are prevalent. Calibration can be used to estimate alternative category scores that are not constrained to be equidistant. For example, a three-point rating scale might be scored 0, 2, and 2.5 to take into account that the distance between the first category and the second category is greater than the distance between the second category and the third category.

Calibration also has many applications in evaluation research. For example, suppose you want to compare four treatments for a duodenal ulcer. The dependent variable is the presence of post-treatment side effects, coded 1 (moderate), 2 (slight), and 3 (none). You can use CHAID's calibration option to estimate scores for the side-effect categories.

This tutorial uses data analyzed by Grizzle et al. (1969), in which the treatment categories represent the amount of the stomach that is surgically removed. The treatment categories are 3/4 resection (G), 1/2 resection and vagotomy (H), 1/4 resection and vagotomy (A), and drainage and vagotomy only (D). The data are shown in Table 5.1.

To perform the calibration, you must choose a predictor variable to be used as an instrument. The instrument should be a variable that is believed to be associated with the dependent variable. We'll use the treatment variable as the instrument.

**Table 5.1 Side-effects data**

| Treatment | Outcome | Cell frequency |
|---|---|---|
| G | Moderate | 16 |
| G | Slight | 38 |
| G | None | 53 |
| H | Moderate | 12 |
| H | Slight | 40 |
| H | None | 58 |
| A | Moderate | 13 |
| A | Slight | 23 |
| A | None | 68 |
| D | Moderate | 7 |
| D | Slight | 28 |
| D | None | 61 |

## Estimating Scores for All Categories

If all category scores for an ordinal dependent variable are unknown, you can use maximum-likelihood calibration to estimate dependent variable scores that are most likely to be associated with a particular predictor variable.

To estimate scores for the side-effect categories:

1. Open the File menu and select Open. Highlight the analysis file *gsk.chd* provided on your CHAID diskette.

❷ Open the Method menu and select Ordinal. A list of default scores appears, as shown in Figure 5.9. These scores are the numeric values for the side-effects variable.

**Figure 5.9 Default category scores**

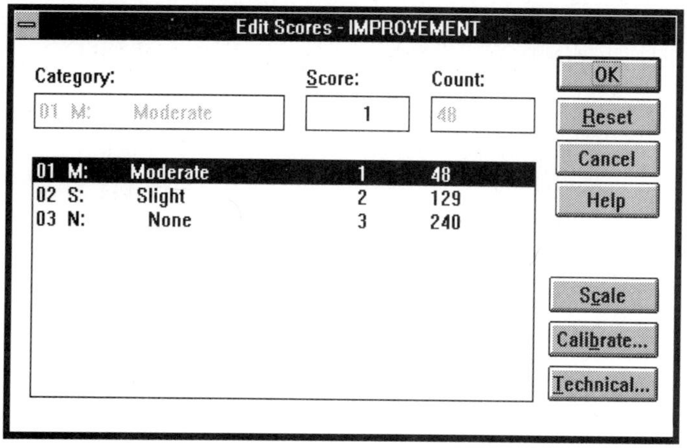


❸ Click on Calibrate.... CHAID displays the Select Instrument to Calibrate dialog box, as shown in Figure 5.10.

**Figure 5.10 Select Instrument to Calibrate dialog box**

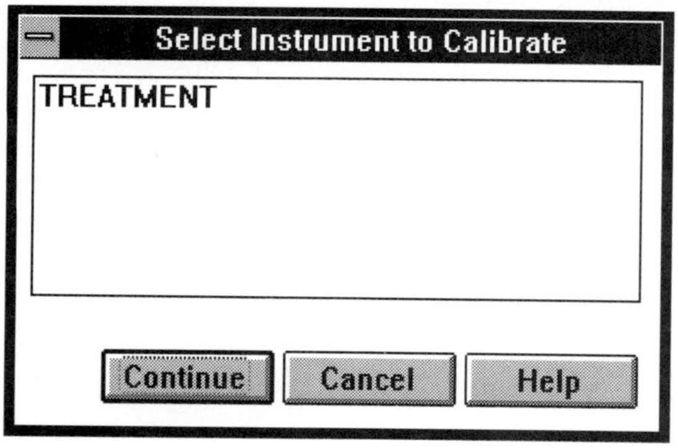


❹ Highlight TREATMENT, the only predictor, and click on Continue.

❺ CHAID displays the estimated scores for the three categories: moderate side effects (22.9), slight side effects (0), and no side effects (100).

❻ To scale these scores so that the score for the no-side-effects category is 0 rather than 100, click on Scale.

CHAID displays the new scores, as shown in Figure 5.11. (See Appendix B for a discussion about uniqueness of scores.)

**Figure 5.11 Unsmoothed category scores**

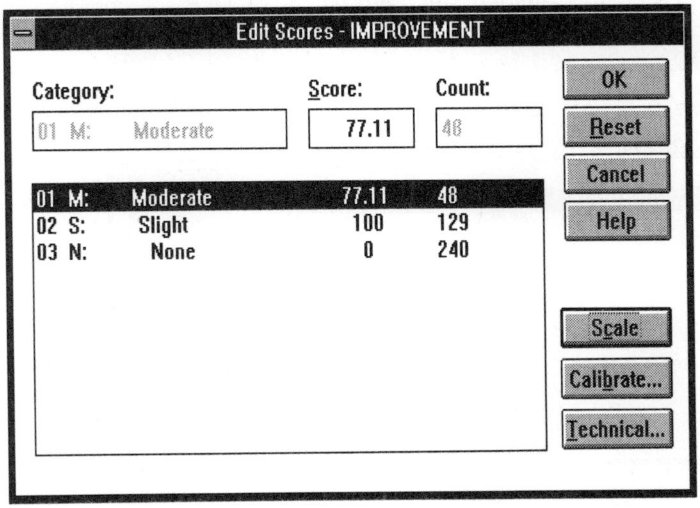


Note that these scores are not ordered from high to low. In CHAID, calibration may be performed in either a smoothed or an unsmoothed form. The smoothed form should be used when you know that your specified category ordering is correct. To force the estimated scores to be properly ordered, you must turn on the Smoothing option.

## Obtaining Smoothed Scores

To obtain smoothed scores:

1. Select Technical in the Edit Scores dialog box.
2. When the Technical Options dialog box appears, select Score Smoothing and click on Continue.
3. Select Calibrate... from the submenu and TREATMENT from the Predictor Selection menu once again.

The Score submenu now shows scores of 0 for "MS" (a joint category of moderate and slight side effects) and 100 for the no-side-effects category. CHAID assigns the same score to moderate and slight side effects to preserve the proper ordering of the categories. Since these two categories have the same score, they are merged.

4. Select Scale from the Edit Scores submenu to scale the scores so that the no-side-effects category has a score of 0 rather than 100. The Score submenu contains the new scores, as shown in Figure 5.12.

**Figure 5.12 Smoothed category scores**

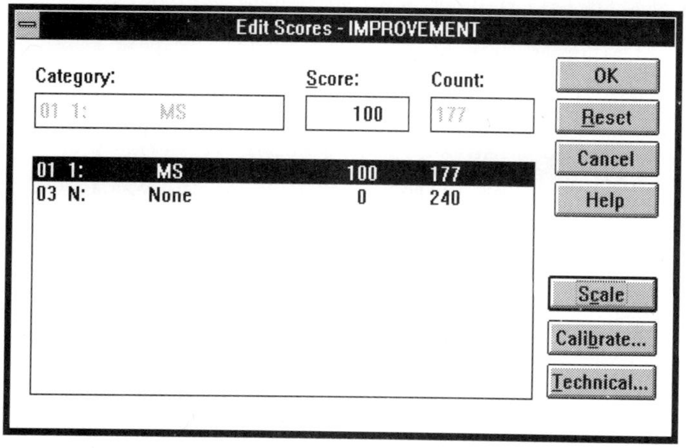


5. Select OK.
6. Open the Tree menu and select Auto to generate the tree. Note that the treatment effect is statistically significant ($p = 0.04$). (This can be seen by opening the Tree menu and selecting Select.)The tree diagram is shown in Figure 5.13.

**Figure 5.13 Tree diagram for treatment**

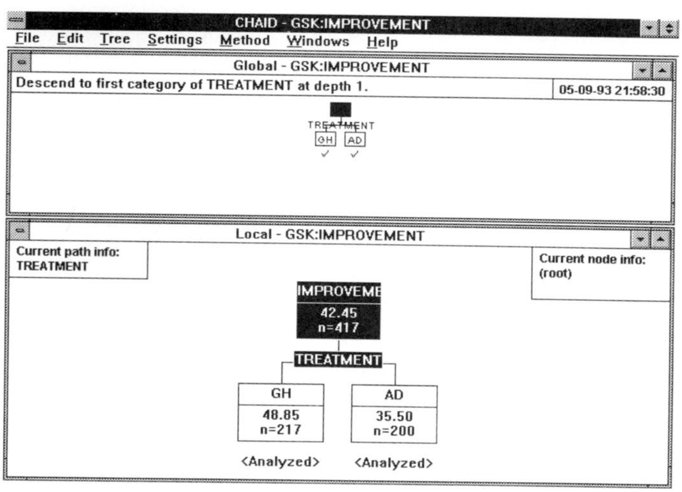

Notice that CHAID merged treatments G and H and treatments A and D. Under the G and H treatments, 48.85% of the patients experienced side effects, compared to only 35.50% of patients who received treatment A or D. Thus, surgical removal of 1/2 or 3/4 of the stomach is significantly more likely to result in side effects than removal of 1/4 or none of the stomach (when removal is performed with the drainage and vagotomy medical procedures).

In the preceding analysis, treatment was defined as a free variable. If the variable were defined as monotonic, the result would have been even more statistically significant, with a $p$ value of 0.017. You can verify this by changing the type setting of the treatment predictor to monotonic under File New. (The results are statistically significant only when smoothing is used.) For further discussion and related analyses of these data, see Agresti (1984) and Magidson (1992, 1993a). See Appendix B for technical details of the single-factor calibration model that is used to estimate these scores.

When you use unsmoothed calibration (the default calibration option), the resulting scores may not be in order (from high to low or low to high) but may instead imply a new category ordering. You should use unsmoothed calibration if you believe that the dependent variable categories can be ordered in a meaningful way but you are unsure about the ordering of one or more categories. In an exploratory analysis, you can examine the scores and the implied category ordering from both forms of calibration (as well as the corresponding fit statistics) and either accept one set of scores or use them to determine how to modify the initial scores.

As a second example, let's say that you have a continuous variable measured using a discrete ordinal scale (that is, the variable has been measured as discrete). For many discretized variables, the distances between the first and second categories, and between the last and next-to-last categories, are greater than the distance between adjacent inner categories. This phenomenon, known as a **floor effect** or a **ceiling effect**, occurs because the average score based on a tail of the distribution may contain extreme scores. In such a case, the commonly used Likert scale, which assumes equal distances between categories, may give misleading results. You can use CHAID's calibration option to estimate the distances between the categories.

## How to Impute Category Scores

If you know scores for all categories of the dependent variable except for a category containing missing values, you should assign the known scores in the usual way. You can omit cases in the missing category, or you can tell CHAID to impute the score for the missing category. CHAID will prompt you for a predictor to use as the instrument.

For example, let's say that you have a variable *income* that is categorized into \$5,000 intervals from \$15,000 through \$50,000, and incomes greater than \$50,000 are grouped into a single category (\$50,000+). The seven lower categories are equally spaced. For example, the distance from the \$15,000–\$19,999 category to the \$20,000–\$24,999 category is the same as the distance from \$25,000–\$29,999 to \$30,000–\$34,999. However, the distance between $45,000–$49,999 and $50,000+ will be considerably larger if the $50,000+ category contains households whose income is extremely high.

As a further example, suppose that persons are categorized according to their score on an exam. If the exam is exceptionally easy, there may be a number of people who receive a perfect score. Thus, some persons included in the highest category would have been included in a much lower category if the exam were more difficult.

In each of the preceding examples, it might be reasonable to hypothesize that the inner categories are equidistant from each other, but the distance between at least one of the end categories and its neighboring category might be greater than the other distances. If all categories were equidistant, consecutive integer scores could be assigned to the categories. For any set of three or more categories known to be equidistant, you can assign any scores to these categories, provided that the difference in the scores of adjacent categories is constant.

The CHAID options for estimating a subset of category scores or calibrating all scores may be used for a CHAID segmentation analysis, or for some other purpose. Our next example shows you how to use imputation.

This tutorial uses two variables from a bivariate normal distribution with a correlation coefficient of 0.50. Table 5.2 is a crosstabulation of these two variables, where the continuous predictor *x* is discretized into three categories using cutoff values of 0 and 1, while the continuous dependent variable *y* is discretized into six categories using the cutoffs 0, 0.5, 1, 1.5, and 2. Both *x* and *y* originally followed a normal distribution with mean 0 and variance 1. The table shows the theoretical probabilities from the bivariate normal distribution multiplied by 10,000. (The total differs from 10,000 because cell entries are rounded to the nearest whole number.)

**Table 5.2 Crosstabulation of discretized bivariate normal x and y with n=10,000**

| | Y | | | | | | |
|---|---|---|---|---|---|---|---|
| **X** | **Less than 0** | **0-0.5** | **0.5-1** | **1-1.5** | **1.5-2** | **Greater than 2** | **Total** |
| Less than 0 | 3,335 | 850 | 505 | 221 | 71 | 20 | 5,002 |
| 0-1 | 1,355 | 765 | 645 | 396 | 178 | 75 | 3,414 |
| Greater than 1 | 310 | 299 | 350 | 301 | 192 | 134 | 1,586 |
| Total | 5,000 | 1,914 | 1,500 | 918 | 441 | 229 | 10,002 |

We will assume that the inner categories of *y* are equidistant and estimate the scores for the categories at the endpoints. To fix the scale, we will use the midpoint of the intervals (0.25, 0.75, 1.25, and 1.75) as the scores for the inner categories. This sets the distance between each of these inner categories to 0.5.

## Estimating Scores for Some Categories

To estimate scores for the first and last categories of *y*:

1. Open the File menu and select Open. Highlight the analysis file *binorm.chd*, which was provided on your installation diskette. CHAID displays the default scores for the six levels of *y*. By default, the first category is highlighted. See Figure 5.14.

**Figure 5.14 Scores for y**

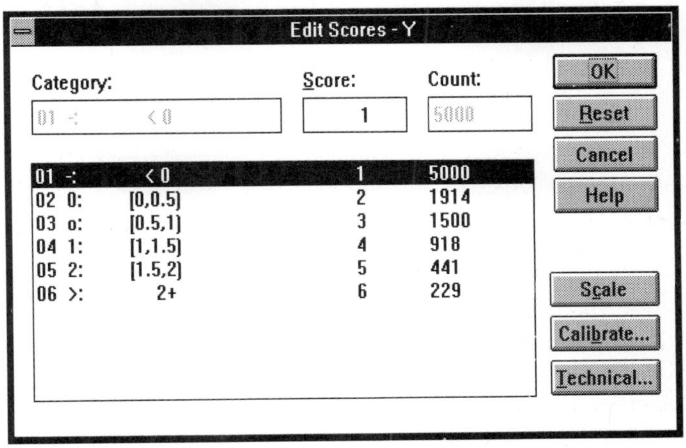


2. For category 01, enter e to indicate that you want to estimate this score.
3. Enter new scores for the remaining categories 2–6:
   0.25
   0.75
   1.25
   1.75
   e
4. Click on OK when you have finished assigning the scores. CHAID prompts you to select a predictor to use as the instrument.
5. Highlight x and then click on Continue. A box appears with the new estimated scores for the categories of *y*, as shown in Figure 5.15.

**Figure 5.15 New scores for y**

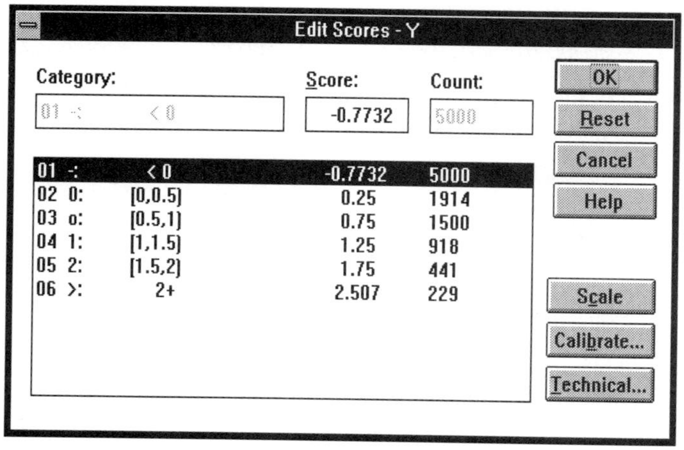


Notice that the categories whose scores we asked CHAID to estimate have been replaced by numerical estimates, while the other scores remain unchanged. Also, while the difference between the scores for the inner categories is still 0.5, the difference between the first two and the last two scores is greater than 0.5. Such results always occur when the data are from a discretized bivariate normal distribution with a non-zero correlation (Goodman, 1984; Goodman, 1991). This suggests that CHAID would be useful in analyzing not only true categorical variables, but also continuous variables that have been discretized.

To show that the assumption of equidistant categories for the inner categories is reasonable, we will now keep the estimated endpoint scores and estimate the inner categories.

1. Move to the second category in the score box.
2. Enter e to indicate that you want to estimate this score.
3. Enter e for categories 3, 4, and 5.
4. Click on OK when you finish assigning the scores.
5. When the Select Instrument to Calibrate dialog box appears, highlight x for the instrument and then click on Continue. A box appears with the scores for the categories of *y*.

Notice how close the estimated scores for the inner categories are to those that we assumed earlier. This result confirms that it is reasonable to assume that the inner categories of *y* are approximately equidistant.

## Controlling the Number of Iterations

Next, we illustrate how to reduce the maximum number of iterations for the ordinal algorithm. We then reestimate the scores for the first and last categories of *y*.

1. In the Edit Scores dialog box, click on Technical to display the Technical Options box.
2. Enter 50 for Maximum iterations to decrease the maximum number of iterations from 100 to 50.
3. Click on Continue.
4. Reenter the scores for the six categories as follows:

e
0.25
0.75
1.25
1.75
e

5. Click on OK, select x as the instrument, and then click on Continue. CHAID warns you that the algorithm did not converge.
6. Click on OK. CHAID displays the new scores, as shown in Figure 5.16.

**Figure 5.16 New category scores**

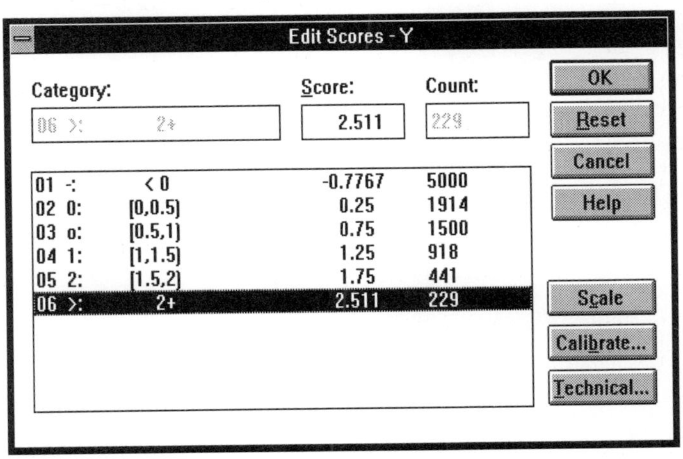


The estimated scores for the end categories (–0.7767 and 2.511) are only approximately the same as the earlier estimates because CHAID did not use enough iterations for the ordinal algorithm to converge to the default epsilon level. For most applications, the default values for epsilon and the maximum number of iterations are sufficient. For further details, see Appendix B.

7. Click on OK; then open the File menu and select Exit to end this CHAID session.

# 6 Reference

## File Menu

Use the File menu, as shown in Figure 6.1, to open, save, delete, and print your analysis file or to exit from CHAID.

**Figure 6.1 File menu**

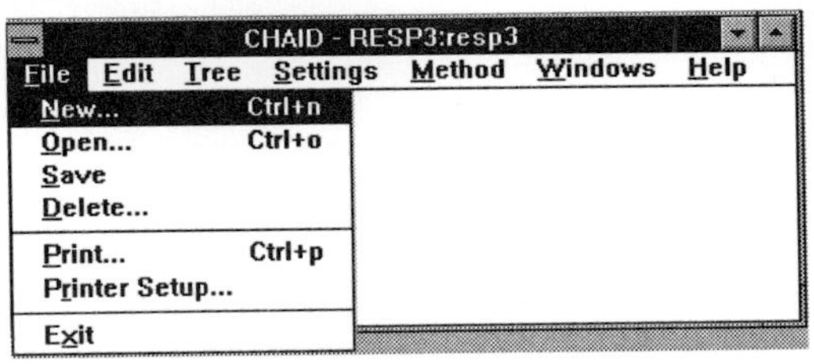


### New

This is used to load an SPSS data file, an ASCII data file, or a binary data file. It is also used to load previously saved CHAID analysis files (they have a *.chd* extension) so that you can change your dependent or predictor variables, predictor combine types and edit variable names and category symbols and labels. If you wish to load a definition (*.def*) file created from an earlier CHAID release, you must first convert the file to a *.chd* analysis file format.

CHAID uses File New to create an analysis file (similar to a definition file in the previous release of CHAID) that defines data files for analysis.

Before an analysis is begun, CHAID scans your data file to count the number of different categories for each predictor variable and record any quantitative values for a frequency or weight variable or for dependent variable category scores; CHAID also counts the number of categories for the dependent variable. After a successful scan, CHAID creates a new file (the analysis file) containing a compressed data file of the designated predictors and dependent variable together with variable names, category labels, and settings for the various parameters.

Using SPSS/PC+ system files or SPSS for Windows data files relieves the user of many definition details, since CHAID is able to make use of SPSS data dictionary items, such as variable names, value labels, and user-missing value definitions. With unstructured "flat" files, such as ASCII or binary, the user must supply CHAID with an equivalent description of the contents of such data files. The description should include the number of fields or variables and the coding method or data type (numbers or character strings) of the individual fields.

After the first analysis of a data file, you can use File Open for subsequent analyses on the same set of variables if your subsequent analysis utilizes the same dependent variable, or a new dependent variable formed by combining or eliminating particular categories of the original dependent variable (see "Method Menu" on p. 109).

## Loading Files

To load a file, choose

File
 New...

This opens the Select New Data to Analyze dialog box, as shown in Figure 6.2.

**Figure 6.2 Select New Data to Analyze dialog box**

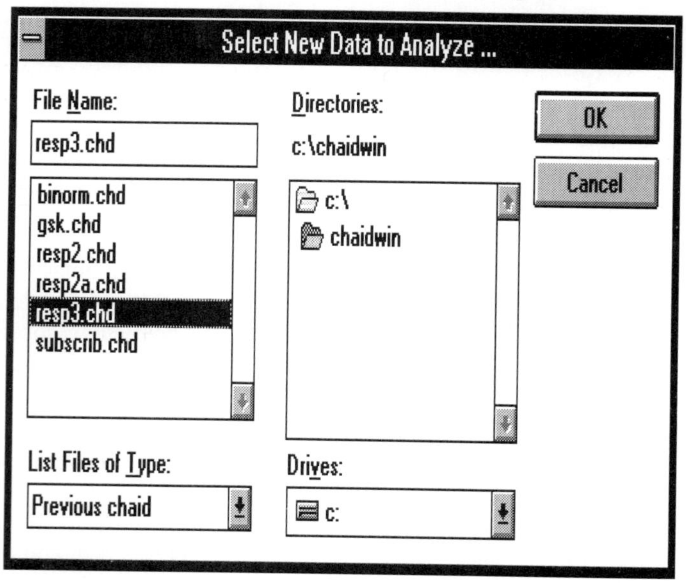

**File Name**. You can type in a filename, a path and filename, or a wildcard search. By default, CHAID looks for all files in the current directory with extensions of *.sav* or *.por* and displays them on the Files list. All files in the directory that match the wildcard search appear on the Files list.

**List Files of Type**. To specify the type of data file that will be loaded, you can choose one of the following alternatives:

**SPSS system files**. Loads SPSS system or portable files. The default is all files with a *.sav*, *.sys*, or *.por* extension.

**User-defined**. Loads ASCII or binary data files. The default extension is *.dat*.

**Previous CHAID.** Loads previous CHAID analysis files. The default extension is *.chd*.

**Directories**. To change directories, select the directory on the Directories list. The main directory is listed first, with subdirectories listed underneath (and indented slightly).

**Drives.** To change drives, select the drive on the Drives list.

## Reading Data Files

**CHAID Analysis File**. The CHAID analysis file (which has an extension of *.chd*) is created by CHAID automatically when a scan has been completed. It saves your data, settings, and options as you defined them for your analysis so that you can retrieve the analysis file for subsequent analyses without the need to set up a new analysis from scratch. Optionally, you can save the tree diagram at the end of an analysis so that it too may be retrieved at a later time for further analysis.

The *.chd* file is actually a pointer to several files that are also saved with the *.chd* file. These files have extensions of *.ch0, .chv, .chu, .chx,* and *.chw*. Included among these files is a compressed copy of the data file that was used for the analysis. Depending on the size of your data file, these files can become quite large. You can use the file management capabilities of CHAID to remove outdated analysis files (see "Delete" on p. 85).

A CHAID analysis file can be loaded from File Open if you wish to continue a previous analysis. File New should be used when you wish to change such things as your dependent variable, predictors and predictor combine types. When using File New, the original source data file must still exist.

Upon opening a CHAID analysis file, the Assign Variables dialog box will appear. Variable settings will appear as they were initially defined.

**CHAID Definition File**. If you wish to load a definition (*.def*) file created from an earlier CHAID release, you must first convert the file to a *.chd* file format outside the CHAID program and then load the file as you would a CHAID analysis file (see above).

Special rules for converting definition files (*.def*) from an earlier CHAID release are:

1. Rename file to end with *.chd* suffix.
2. The first line of the file should be ".id." A blank space must follow ".id."
3. Any print options must be removed. Print options begin with "Print" on one line, followed by the options on another line, and "End" on the last line. Delete all of these lines.
4. The original source data file, referenced by the definition file, must still exist.
5. The converted file must be loaded through File New and rescanned. Loading through File Open will cause errors.

**SPSS Files.** SPSS/PC+ system files, SPSS for Windows data files, and SPSS portable files are data files saved through the SPSS program.

You can start CHAID with an SPSS file either from within SPSS or from the Windows Main menu.

## Starting CHAID from SPSS

Within SPSS, open the Statistics menu and select SPSS CHAID. If you have a **working data file** (a data file currently open), CHAID uses that working data file and brings you into the Assign Variables dialog box.

## Opening an SPSS File in CHAID

If you are already running CHAID (or if you started CHAID from SPSS with no working data file), use the following steps to open an SPSS/PC+ system file, SPSS for Windows data file, or SPSS portable data file:

1. Open the File menu and select New. All files in the current directory with *.sav* or *.por* extensions will be displayed.
2. Select one of these files. Upon opening a SPSS file, the Assign Variables dialog box will appear. Variables defined in the SPSS file will be listed in the Variables box.

**SPSS Variable Labels.** If your original SPSS file contains variable labels, these labels will appear throughout your analysis.

- For the dependent variable, the variable label will appear in the caption line of the Edit Scores dialog box.
- When rearranging a predictor, the variable label will appear in the caption line of the Rearrange Categories dialog box.
- In both Tree Select and Settings Variable Categories, variable labels will appear for the highlighted predictor.
- Variable labels will also be printed as part of the documentation file.

**SPSS Weight Variable.** If your SPSS file has a weight variable defined, that variable appears automatically in the Frequency Variable box. You can remove it if you do not want the same case replication applied in CHAID that was applied in SPSS.

## User-defined Data Files

User-defined data files can be either ASCII text files or fixed-length binary files. In ASCII text files, lines of printable characters are terminated with CR/LF control characters. In fixed-length binary files, each record has exactly the same number of characters, and records are not terminated with a CR/LF character sequence. An ASCII file can be either **column-oriented** (fixed-field format) or **delimited** (freefield format). Binary files are always column-oriented.

An example of an ASCII file format with a delimiter is the *binorm.dat* file provided on the CHAID installation disk. The delimiter for this file is a blank space. Figure 6.3 shows a partial listing of this file:

**Figure 6.3 Partial listing of an ASCII file**

```
1 1 3335
1 2 850
1 3 505
1 4 221
1 5 71
1 6 20
2 1 1355
2 2 765
2 3 645
2 4 396
2 5 178
2 6 75
3 1 310
```

Upon opening a User-defined file, the Define Variables dialog box appears, as shown in Figure 6.4.

## Defining Variables

The Define Variables dialog box, as shown in Figure 6.4, is used to define variables from an ASCII or Binary data file.

**Figure 6.4 Define Variables dialog box**

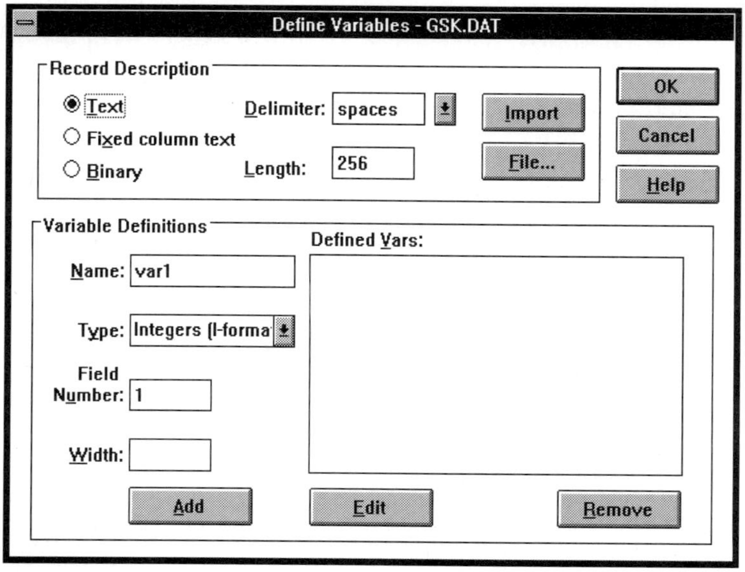


**Record Description.** Choose one of the file type alternatives listed. (Remember that the correct file type should be set before defining variables in order to prevent any misinterpretation by CHAID.)

- **Text.** Freefield format ASCII files with a delimiter. The variables are recorded in the same order for each case but not necessarily in the same locations. You must specify the delimiter that separates data values in the Delimiter box to the right and also the Field Number.
- **Fixed column text.** Fixed-format ASCII files. You must specify the Start Column and Width values for each variable. Each variable is recorded in the same column location on the same record line for each case in the data file.
- **Binary.** Fixed-length binary files. Each variable is recorded in the same column location on the same record line for each case in the data file. It is vitally important to fill in the record length value ("Length") as CHAID has no other way of knowing what constitutes a record.
- **Delimiter.** For ASCII text files.The default is a blank space ("spaces"). You may also enter: 1) the words `comma` or `tabs`; 2) any single character; or 3) a decimal number

that represents the ASCII code of the desired delimiter character. For example, 47 would specify "/" for your delimiter.

**Length**. Enter a value equal to or greater than the maximum record (line) length in the data file. The default is 256. If the specified value is less than the maximum line length, an error results. You must fill in the exact record length for all binary files. For ASCII files, the length need only be filled in if it is larger than the default.

## Importing Data Files

Select Import to import ASCII text files with a delimiter. Errors will occur if you attempt to import analysis files or SPSS files. This option automatically fills in variable definitions in the Variable Definitions box. A partial listing of your input data file will appear on the screen. Each individual record (or row) from your original data file is read in as a column. Thus, column 1 contains a complete record as defined by each field listed. If the first line of your data file contains variable names, select the Use First Line as Names option to have CHAID read in the variable names.

After importing a data file, you should check the Define Variables dialog box to make sure the variables have been defined correctly (especially the type).

## Changing Data Files

Select File to change the input data file. The current data file name is shown on the main bar of the Define Variables dialog box.

If variables have been previously defined, the new data file must have the same form in order to be read correctly. If the form is not exactly the same, use Edit to specify any changes. The File option is especially useful if you have two data files with the same setup and variable definitions, but containing different values.

For example, if the same survey was given to two different groups of people in January and in June, the two different groups of respondents would be asked the same questions, but their responses would be different. Thus, the January and June data sets would have the same variables, but different data values.

Instead of having to separately load each file through File New and specifying variable definitions and category labels twice, you need only do this for the first data set and scan the data file to produce a *.chd* file. Then, 1) use File New to reload the *.chd* file into the Assign Variables dialog box, 2) select Define Variables to open the Define Variables dialog box, and 3) select File to change the data file name to the second data set. All variable definitions will remain.

Just remember to change the save filename when you rescan the data so as not to overwrite the previous file. This option is only available for analysis files that have an ASCII or binary data file as its original source.

## Entering Variable Definitions

For each variable, the following information must be defined:

**Name**. Type in the name of each variable (up to 15 characters); otherwise CHAID will provide a name (such as *var1*).

**Type**. The default value is Integers. In order for CHAID to read your data file correctly, these options must be set correctly for each variable.

There are three options for ASCII text or fixed column text file types:

| | |
|---|---|
| **Char (Str)** | *Interpret field as a string variable, that is, no conversion takes place.* |
| **Integers (Nbr)** | *Interpret field as an integer.* |
| **Reals (Real)** | *Interpret field as real number.* Specify this option when a variables values contain decimals. |

There are also three options for Binary file types:

| | |
|---|---|
| **Binary Int (Real A1)** | *A binary integer field.* The length field must be 1, 2, or 4. |
| **Binary Flt (Real A4)** | *A binary IEEE single precision floating point field.* The field must always occupy four bytes in the data record. |
| **Binary Dbl (Real A8)** | *A binary IEEE double precision (eight bytes) floating point field.* The field must always occupy eight bytes in the data record. (Dbl is also the type used by SPSS data files for numeric values.) |

**Field Number/Start Column**. For ASCII text files with a delimiter, enter the field number for a variable. For ASCII fixed column and Binary file types, enter the column that a variable begins in.

**Width**. The number of columns that a variable uses. Does not apply to ASCII text files with a delimiter.

For ASCII text files, the field number for a variable is where fields are determined by the delimiter. Thus, for the ASCII file in Figure 6.3, the number 3,335 would have a field number of 3.

For fixed column or binary file types, Start Column and Width must be specified for each variable in order for CHAID to read the data file correctly. For example, if your first variable is in positions 1–5 in your file, you would specify a start column of 1 and a width of 5. The next variable in your file might be in positions 6–7. In this case, you would specify a start column of 6 and a width of 2.

To enter a variable definition:

1. Specify the variable name, type, and, if necessary, field number/start column and width.
2. Click on Add. The variable name, number, and data type appear on the Defined Vars list. Only variables listed on the Defined Vars list will be eligible to be included in the analysis.

The following general rules apply:

1. You can enter variables in any order.
2. You can specify multiple variables in the same or overlapping column locations.
3. You can read selective data fields or records. You don't have to define or read all the data in the file. CHAID reads only the columns and records you specify and skips over any data you don't define.

## Editing and Removing Variable Definitions

In order to change the required information (such as the name, start column, etc.) for a variable in the Define Variables dialog box, highlight the variable name, click on Edit, make any desired changes, and then click on Replace to change the information (or Restore to restore the variable to its original settings).

In order to prevent a variable in the Define Variables dialog box from being read when CHAID creates the analysis data file, highlight the variable name and then click on Remove.

Upon clicking on OK, CHAID will take you to the Assign Variables dialog box, as shown in Figure 6.5.

## Assigning Variables

Use the Assign Variables dialog box, as shown in Figure 6.5, to assign variables and set options for your analysis.

**Figure 6.5 Assign Variables dialog box**

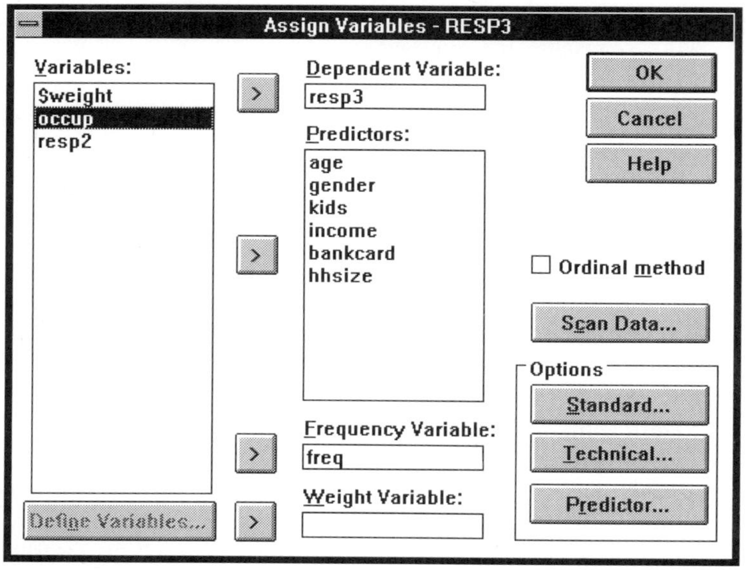


## Variable Designation

All eligible variables that may be included in the analysis are listed on the Variables list. Variables may be designated as one of four types: dependent variable, predictors, frequency variable, or weight variable. One dependent and at least one predictor must be specified in order to begin an analysis. To select a variable, highlight the variable name and then click on the appropriate arrow button to move the variable name into the corresponding box.

**Dependent Variable.** Assign one variable to be used as the dependent variable.

**Predictors**. Assign one or more variables to be used as predictors.

**Frequency Variable**. Assign one variable to be used as a frequency variable (optional).

**Weight Variable.** Assign one variable to be used as a weight variable (optional).

(See “Frequency Variable” on p. 8 and “Weight Variable” on p. 9 for further details regarding the use of frequency and weight variables.)

To deselect a variable, highlight the variable name in either the Dependent Variable, Predictors, Frequency, or the Weight Variable box, and click on the reverse arrow. The variable moves back onto the variable list.

The following option is also available:

- **Ordinal method**. Select ordinal method if the dependent variable categories are to be treated as ordered. See "Ordinal" on p. 111 for further details. If you select this option, it is recommended you choose Edit Scores as your startup mode in order to view or edit your dependent variable category scores before your analysis is begun. Startup mode can be specified by clicking on Standard.

**Define Variables**. Click on Define Variables... to return to the Define Variables box. This option is available only if you begin with an ASCII, binary, or CHAID analysis data file.

## Scanning

Select Scan Data to create an analysis file (*.chd* file). A scan counts up the number of categories for each variable designated as dependent or predictor variable and makes use of any frequency or weight variables to create the proper type of analysis file for your input data file. A scan needs to be performed before beginning a CHAID analysis. If Scan Data has not been selected, a scan will automatically be performed by CHAID before an analysis is begun.

Scanning your data beforehand is useful in determining if CHAID has read your input data file correctly. After a scan has taken place, you may edit category symbols and labels and check category counts for accuracy.

To scan your data beforehand, click on Scan Data to open the Save As dialog box, as shown in Figure 6.6, to specify the filename (analysis run name) for this analysis, such as *resp2*. If you are having trouble scanning your data a second time (when you select Scan Data, the Scan Results box pops up), deselect any variable and then reselect it before selecting Scan Data again.

**Figure 6.6 Save As dialog box**

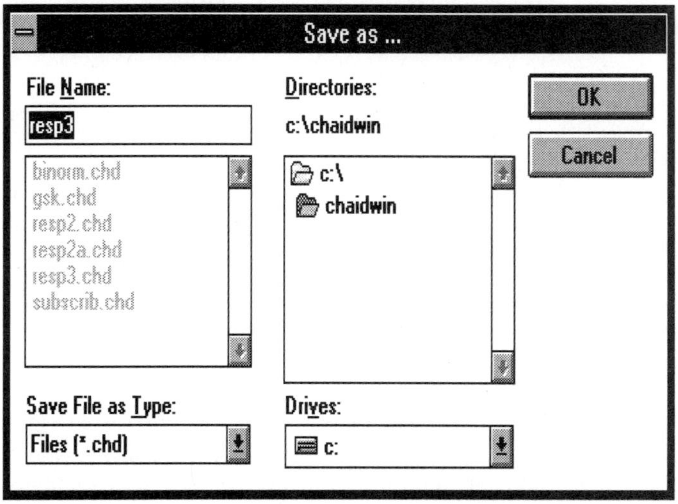


The file saved will have a *.chd* extension. You may also use the file list, Directories, and Drives boxes to select a previous filename, in which case CHAID will prompt you if you want to overwrite the file.

After specifying the save name, click on OK. CHAID will scan the data file and then open the Scan Messages dialog box.

## Scan Messages

The Scan Messages dialog box, as shown in Figure 6.7, informs you of any errors that may have occurred during the scan process.

**Figure 6.7 Scan Messages dialog box**

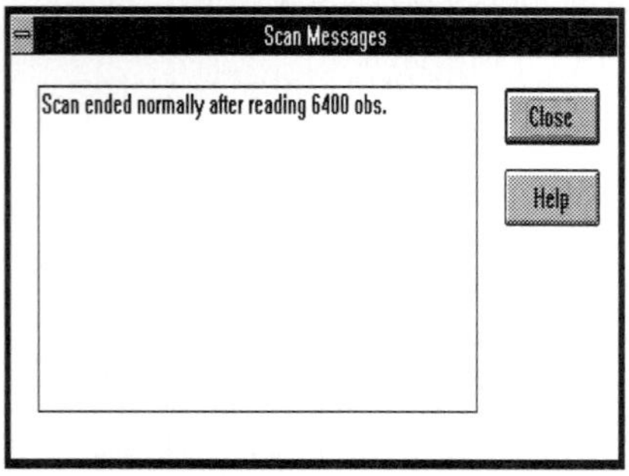

Among the more likely error situations are:

- Specifying a nonexistent input data file
- Failure to identify the dependent variable
- Failure to identify at least one predictor
- Specifying a variable that has only one category or that has more than the maximum 31
- Specifying an incorrect file type

Other more exotic situations, such as the inability to write certain temporary files, are likely to be caused by insufficient disk space or lack of write access to a disk. Other conditions are checked and displayed as either informational or warning messages. CHAID will be able to carry out an analysis in these cases, but be careful, the conditions may be symptomatic of more subtle errors.

Informational messages include detailing the number of lines read, lines used, and seconds used to complete the scan.

After a successful scan, clicking on Close will open the Scan Results dialog box.

## Scan Results

The Scan Results dialog box, as shown in Figure 6.8, contains a listing of all the variables along with predictor combine type, automatic eligibility, merge level, and number of categories. The predictor list contains symbols, labels, and frequency counts for each category of the variable listed in the Variable box. You may edit category labels and examine frequency counts for accuracy.

**Figure 6.8 Scan Results dialog box**

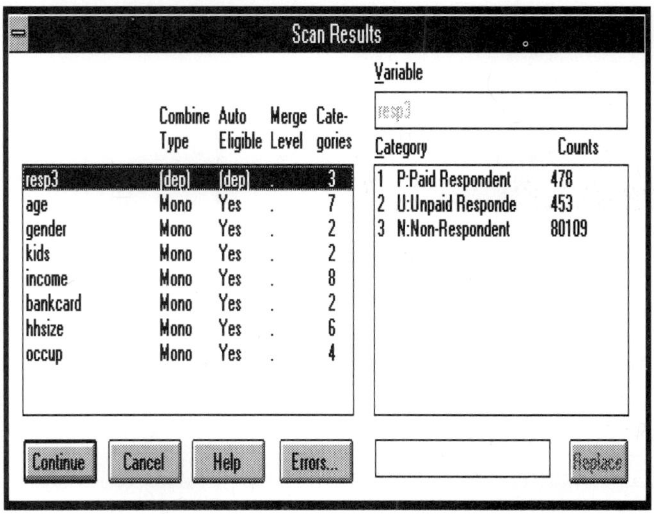

## Editing Category Labels

To edit category labels, highlight a variable name. The variable name appears in the Variable box. Next, highlight the category you wish to change in the Category box. Type in your new label in the text box next to the Replace button in the bottom right corner. You may also type in a new symbol and label in the format: “symbol: label.”

Symbols may be one character in length. Labels may be up to 15 characters in length.

- Select Replace to accept an edited label.
- Select Errors to return to the Scan Messages dialog box.

## Options

**Standard**. Click on Standard... to change options such as depth limit, subgroup sizes, merge and eligibility levels, and startup mode. (See “Options” on p. 102 for more details.)

**Technical**. Click on Technical... to change various technical parameters regarding your analysis. (See “Technical” on p. 104 for more details.)

**Predictor**. Click on Predictor... to open the Predictor Options dialog box, as shown in Figure 6.9, which allows you to specify predictor combine type, individual predictor merge levels, and whether or not a variable should be used in an automatic analysis.

**Figure 6.9 Predictor Options dialog box**

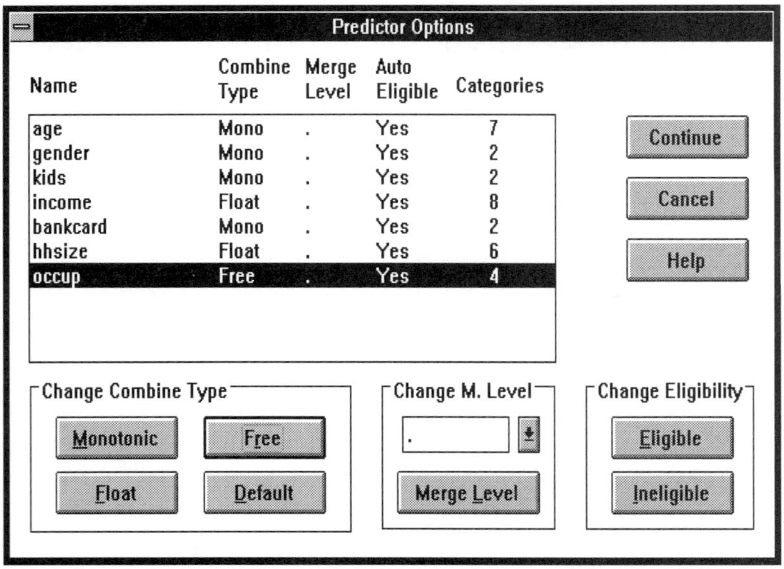

**Change Combine Type**. Use the Predictor Options dialog box (Figure 6.9) to specify a type for each predictor. The predictor type specifies how categories of a predictor may be combined.

CHAID predictors can be classified as follows:

**Monotonic**. Only adjacent categories may be combined. Used when the predictor categories are known to be ordered.

**Float**. The same as monotonic except that the last category (often one that reflects a type of "missing" value) can be combined with any other category.

**Free**. Categories may be combined whether or not they are adjacent to each other. Used when predictor categories have no natural ordering.

**Default**. If no specific type has been filled in, the predictor will be assumed by CHAID to be monotonic (unless one of the categories has an SPSS missing-value setting, in which case, the default is float).

Following are examples of predictor types:

- If variable *SPEED* (three categories: low, medium, and high) were declared to be monotonic, the categories low and high would be able to merge only if low first merged with medium, or high first merged with medium.
- If variable *SPEED* were declared to be a free variable, the low and high categories would be allowed to merge, as would any of the categories.
- Float indicates a monotonic variable whose last category can combine freely with any of the others. An example of a float variable is the common five-point scale (1 = strongly agree, 2 = somewhat agree, 3 = neither agree nor disagree, 4 = somewhat disagree, 5 = strongly disagree) with a sixth category for nonresponse or missing. By specifying this variable to be a six category float variable, it is treated as a monotonic variable except that the "missing" category could be merged with any of the others.

For variables with only two categories, all three combine types are equivalent, since there is only one way in which the categories can combine. Therefore, it is unnecessary to specify a type for predictors with only two categories.

To specify predictors to be of a certain type, highlight the variable name, and then click on the type (Monotonic, Free, or Float). The type will appear in the Combine Type column. You may use the click-and-drag technique or ctrl-click to highlight more than one variable at a time.

**Change Merge Level**. The user can control the level of difficulty of combining categories for a specific predictor by specifying a predictor-specific merge level. The higher the level, the more difficult it will be for categories of this predictor to be combined. If a level of 1.00 is specified, no categories will be merged for that predictor.

To set a predictor-specific merge level, type in a number between 0 and 1 in the Change M. Level box above the Merge Level button, highlight a variable name, and click on Merge Level. You may use the click-and-drag technique or ctrl-click to highlight more than one variable at a time. A period (.) represents the default value.

If no merge level is specified, the default merge level specified in the Standard Options dialog box is used. Any predictor-specific merge level overrides the merge level specified in the Standard Options dialog box.

**Change Eligibility**. **Automatic eligibility** refers to whether or not a variable is to be considered for use in an analysis that is run in automatic startup mode (specified under "Eligibility Level" on p.103). The default value for all variables is Yes.

To exclude a variable from being used in the automatic analysis, highlight the variable name, and then click on Ineligible in the Change Eligibility box. The status of each variable is listed in the Auto Eligible column. No signifies that a variable is ineligible.

## Open

**Opening Files.**To open a previously saved CHAID analysis file, either to continue the analysis from the point at which the file was saved or to start a new analysis, choose

File
 Open...

This opens the Select Input File dialog box, as shown in Figure 6.10.

**Figure 6.10 Select Input File dialog box**

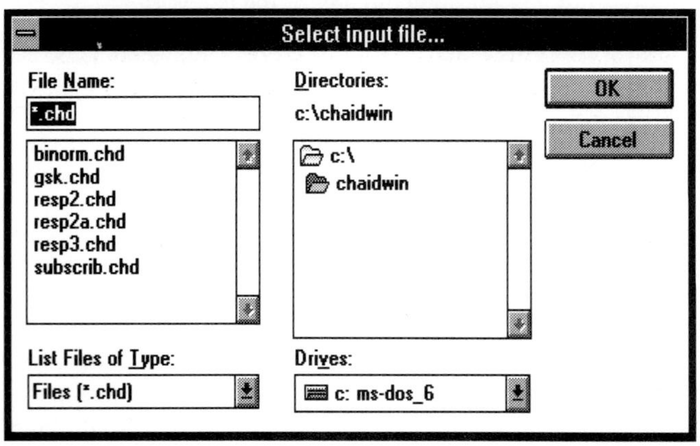


If the file you want to use is not a CHAID analysis file, you must first use File New to define the file for CHAID analysis.

**File Name**. You can type in a filename, a path and filename, or a wildcard search. By default, CHAID looks for all files in the current directory with the extension of *.chd* and displays them on the files list. All files in the directory that match the wildcard search appear on the files list.

**Directories**. To change directories, select the directory on the Directories list. The main directory is listed first with subdirectories listed underneath (and indented slightly).

**Drives**. To change drives, select the drive on the Drives list.

**List Files of Type**. No options are available other than the default.

Upon specifying a usable CHAID filename, you have the choice of retrieving the previously saved tree at the point at which it was last saved or starting the analysis over. (If you did not use File Save to save the tree previously, CHAID will automatically start over the analysis.)

## Save

Used to save the current CHAID analysis file at the current point in the analysis. The saved file takes the analysis run name with a *.chd* extension. The run name is listed together with the dependent variable name at the top and center of the screen. Analysis run names are specified when you scan your data file.

## Delete

Used to delete any file(s) you specify. When you select Delete from the File menu, you can change drives and directories and search for and select files from the file list, just as you do when opening a file (see "Open" on p. 84).

CHAID analysis files may take up a lot of space. Once there is no need to keep a *.chd* file, you should delete it. When you delete a *.chd* file, all accompanying files (with extensions of *.ch0, .chu, .chv, .chw,* and *.chx*) are also deleted.

## Print

To print output, choose

File
 Print...

This opens up the Print Selection dialog box, as shown in Figure 6.11. You may print five different types of output: tree diagrams, crosstabulations (Tables), documentation, gains charts and predictor significance listings (Predictor).

**Figure 6.11 Print Selections dialog box**

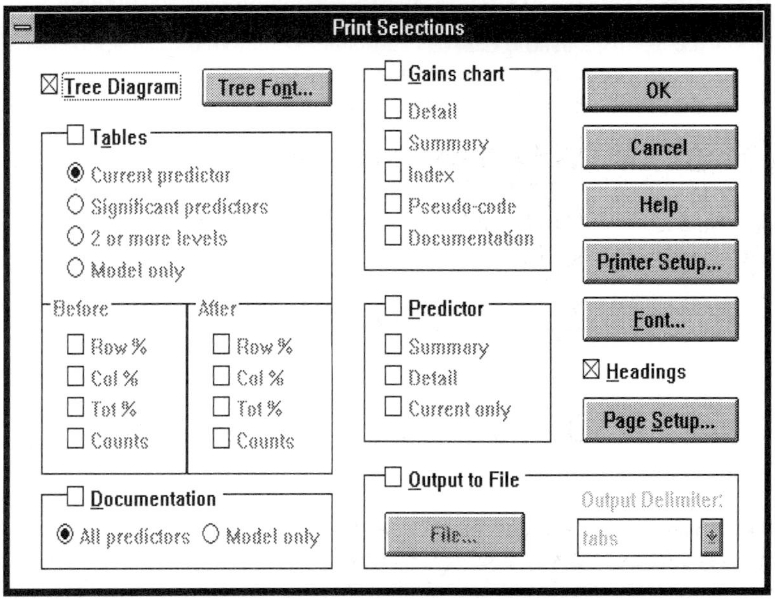


- **Tree Diagram**. Use this option to print the current local tree diagram. If your tree diagram is too large to fit on one page, CHAID will print the tree on separate pages that may be then pasted together by hand. If the bottom or side of a page contains an incomplete tree node(s), CHAID will begin the next page by printing that particular node(s) in complete form.

  As an alternative, you may select Tree Font... to attempt to make the tree fit on fewer pages by changing the font, font style, or font size.

- **Tables.** Use this option to print a crosstabulation of the predictor (rows) by the dependent variable (columns).

  Once Tables has been selected, you need to choose from one of the following alternatives in the Tables box to determine which tables to print:

  - **Current predictor**. Produces tables only for the current predictor (that is, the predictor name that is highlighted in the Local window, which is the predictor used to split the current "parent" node).

  - **Significant predictors**. Produces tables for all predictor variables that were statistically significant at the current tree level.

❍ **2 or more levels.** Produces tables for all predictor variables except those for which all categories were merged together at the current tree level. (This selection produces tables for all significant predictors plus others.)

❍ **Model only.** Produces tables for only those variables included in the current model (that is, those predictor variables included on the current tree diagram).

## Table Options

The following table options are available. (You may choose as many options as you wish.) There are two different types of options. The first type of option deals with category merging. Tables can be produced before and/or after category merging.

**Before.** Use this option to produce a crosstabulation of the current predictor by the dependent variable before category merging takes place.

**After.** Use this option to produce a crosstabulation of the current predictor by the dependent variable after category merging has taken place. If no categories were merged by CHAID, this option will produce the same tables as the Before option. For the predictor variable, category symbols (instead of labels) are displayed in order to conserve space.

The second type of option deals with the type of percentage (or frequency counts) to be produced.

❑ **Row %.** Table entries for each row will be the conditional percentage distribution of the dependent variable. The percentages within each row sum to 100%. If the ordinal method is in use, the last column of the table will contain the average score and the individual dependent variable category scores will appear at the bottom of the table in a row titled *Scores*.

❑ **Col %.** Table entries for each column will be the percentage distribution of the predictor. The percentages within each column sum to 100%.

❑ **Tot %.** Table entries will be the percentage of the total subgroup.

❑ **Counts.** Table entries will be frequency counts.

When printing from any node other than the root node, CHAID will print information pertaining to the current subgroup that you've printed from. This information contains the tree level, sample size, and variable names and categories for the current path on the tree diagram.

❑ **Documentation.** This option prints a documentation file containing information about the run (the dependent variable categories, category scores (if used), standard and technical parameters, etc.). (See Figure 6.12.) Use this as backup documentation for your CHAID segmentation to help rebuild an analysis that you haven't saved.

In addition, you may choose from one of the following options to determine which predictors should be documented:

- ❍ **All predictors**. Prints a listing of all the predictors.
- ❍ **Model only**. Prints a listing of predictors used to build the current tree diagram.

Predictor lists contain the number of categories each predictor has ("levels"), the predictor combine type (free, monotonic, or float), category symbols and labels, and frequency counts (unweighted and weighted).

**Figure 6.12 Sample of documentation output**

```
CurrDir=C:\CHAIDWIN
FileName=RESP3.CHD
SourceData=SUBSCRIB.SAV

Standard Options                              Technical Options
StartUp=              FirstPred               Method=        Nominal
AnalysisDepth=        2                       Chi-Square=    LikelihoodRatio
MinSubGroup(Before)=  3000                    WLM=           Off
MinSubGroup(After)=   1500                    Bonferroni=    Yes
EligibilityLevel=     0.050
MergeLevel=           0.050
FreqVar=              freq
Weight=               <none>
resp3      levels=3                 (Dependent)
level      value      symbol:       label               frequency
1)         1          P:            Paid Respondent     478
2)         2          U:            Unpaid Responde     453
3)         3          N:            Non-Respondent      80109
hhsize     levels=6                 Floating
1)         1          1:            1                   25384
2)         2          2:            2                   11240
3)         3          3:            3                   4892
4)         4          4:            4                   3187
5)         5          F:            Five or more        3011
6)         6          U:            Unknown             33326
age        levels=7                 Floating
1)         1          1:            18-24               677
2)         2          2:            25-34               3940
3)         3          3:            35-44               4566
4)         4          4:            45-54               3231
5)         5          5:            55-64               2898
6)         6          6:            65+                 7121
7)         7          U:            Unknown             58607
kids       levels=2                 Monotonic
1)         1          Y:            Yes                 6311
2)         2          N:            No                  74729
occup      levels=4                 Free
1)         1          W:            White Collar        4231
2)         2          B:            Blue Collar         3910
3)         3          O:            Other               24029
4)         4          U:            Unknown             48870
bankcard   levels=2                 Monotonic
1)         1          Y:            Yes                 6083
2)         2          N:            No                  74957
gender     levels=2                 Monotonic
1)         1          M:            Male                61313
2)         2          F:            Female              19727
income     levels=8                 Monotonic
1)         1          1:            Under $8,000        11029
2)         2          2:            $8,000-$9,999       4856
3)         3          3:            $10,000-$14,999     10205
4)         4          4:            $15,000-$19,999     9703
5)         5          5:            $20,000-$24,999     7852
6)         6          6:            $25,000-$34,999     15321
7)         7          7:            $35,000-$49,999     13602
8)         8          8:            $50,000 or more     8472
```

❑ **Gains chart**. After selecting Gains chart, you may specify the charts you want printed in the Gains chart box. Charts will be based on the settings specified in the Gains Chart Options dialog box. There are five possible charts that can be produced.

❑ **Detail**. Prints a detailed gains chart. For more information on detailed gains charts, see "Contents" on p. 120.

❑ **Summary**. Prints a summary gains chart. For more information on summary gains charts, see "Summary" on p. 120.

❑ **Index.** Prints the operational definitions of the segments, such as *HHSIZE* = *1* and *INCOME*=*5*, etc. (See Figure 6.13.). Also contains a listing of the segment size and average score for each segment.

**Figure 6.13 Sample of index output**

| id | count | score | vars... | |
|---|---|---|---|---|
| -1- | 2,291 | 4.78 | hhsize=1 | occup=WB |
| -2- | 11,313 | 12.06 | hhsize=1 | occup=O |
| -3- | 11,780 | 24.15 | hhsize=1 | occup=U |
| -4- | 11,240 | 9.57 | hhsize=2 | |
| -5- | 11,090 | 5.52 | hhsize=3-F | |
| -6- | 1,349 | 20.00 | hhsize=U | occup=W-O |
| -7- | 31,977 | 45.71 | hhsize=U | occup=U |

❑ **Pseudo-code**. Prints a series of SPSS "do if... else if..." statements that define the segments, as shown in Figure 6.14. This output could be used by a programmer in a program to assign segment numbers and/or segment scores to individual data records.

**Figure 6.14 Sample of pseudo-code output**

```
do if ( ((hhsize= 1) )).
- do if ( ((1<=occup & occup<=2) )).
- compute chdsegmt = 001 .
- compute chdscore = 4.78 .
- else if ( ((occup= 3) )).
- compute chdsegmt = 002 .
- compute chdscore = 12.06 .
- else if ( ((occup= 4) )).
- compute chdsegmt = 003 .
- compute chdscore = 24.15 .
- else.
- compute chderror = 1 .
- end if.
else if ( ((hhsize= 2) )).
- compute chdsegmt = 004 .
- compute chdscore = 9.57 .
else if ( ((3<=hhsize & hhsize<=5) )).
- compute chdsegmt = 005 .
- compute chdscore = 5.52 .
else if ( ((hhsize= 6) )).
- do if ( ((1<=occup & occup<=3) )).
- compute chdsegmt = 006 .
- compute chdscore = 20.00 .
- else if ( ((occup= 4) )).
- compute chdsegmt = 007 .
- compute chdscore = 45.71 .
- else.
- compute chderror = 2 .
- end if.
else.
- compute chderror = 3 .
end if.
```

- **Documentation**. Prints a documentation file (see above) that relates to the predictors used in producing the gains charts and also includes dependent variable category scores used in calculating the gains charts.
- **Predictor**. Use this option to print information on predictors that are candidates for splitting the current node, as shown in Figure 6.15. Choose from the following options:
  - **Summary**. Prints a listing of predictors that could be used to split the current node. The information printed is the same information that appears in the Select Predictor dialog box when you select Tree Select. The information printed contains the predictor names, *p* values, number of CHAID defined levels ("groups") and corresponding category symbols ("categories"). For example, 6->4 means that after CHAID's merging algorithm was performed, a six-category variable now has only four categories. The grouping of symbols shows you which categories have been merged. This option may be used in conjunction with the Detail option to get more detailed information (see "Detail," below).
  - **Detail**. To be used in conjunction with either the Summary or Current only option. Prints more detailed information regarding predictors, including category symbols and labels and before- and after-merging frequency counts.
  - **Current only**. Used in conjunction with the Detail option to print information only for the current variable. The information printed is the same information that appears in the Variable Categories dialog box when you select Settings Variable Categories.

**Figure 6.15 Sample of predictor output**

```
Size        Variable    Group

6400        <root>
1464        hhsize      1/4      [1] 2 3-F U

predictor   p-value     levels   groups
age         6.3e-20     7->3     1-5 6 U
occup       1.9e-24     4->3     WB O U
bankcard    5.7e-13     2        Y N
gender      0.022       2        M F
```

For any node other than the root node, CHAID also will print out information pertaining to the current subgroup. This information is at the top of the table and contains the tree level, sample size, and variable names and categories associated with the node that is highlighted in the Local window.

The following options are also available:

- **Headings**. Produces a bottom line on all pages of printed output that contains the date, analysis file name, dependent variable name, and list of predictors used in the analysis.

- **Output to File**. All output will be printed to a text file. Selecting Tree Diagram will generate text information with one line of data for each node on the tree diagram This is similar to the history file generated in the original version of CHAID. (See Appendix E for more details.)

  Click on File... to specify the name of the file that CHAID should print to. The Specify Output Text File dialog box will appear. Select a filename from the ones listed or type in your own filename.

  **Output Delimiter**. You may specify a delimiter to be used for the output text file in the Output Delimiter box. The default delimiter is tabs. You may also enter 1) the words `comma` or `spaces` (for blank spaces), 2) any single character, or 3) a decimal number that represents the ASCII code of the desired delimiter character. For example, 47 would specify "/" for your delimiter.

## Margins, Titles, Printer and Font Options

**Page Setup**. Click on Page Setup... to open the Page Setup dialog box, as shown in Figure 6.16, where you can change page margins and enter a title and page numbers to output.

**Figure 6.16 Page Setup dialog box**

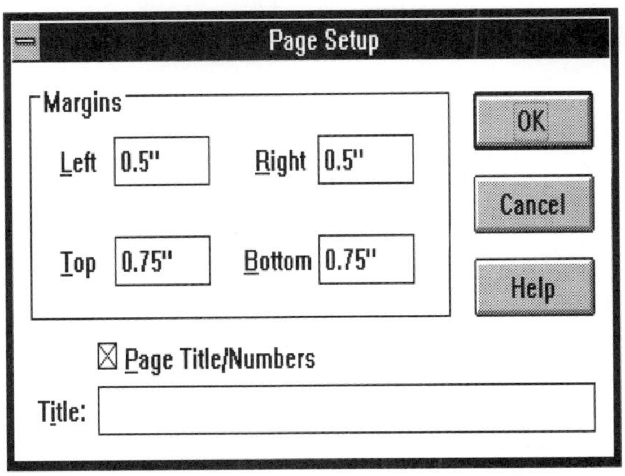


**Margins**. Set page margins for printed output. Margins may be set in inches (") or centimeters (cm). For example, to change the left margin to be 0.25 centimeters, type in "`.25cm`."

- **Page Title/Numbers.** Select Page Title/Numbers to have CHAID print a title and page numbers on each page of output.

**Title.** Type in the title that you wish to appear at the top of each output page. The title can have up to 144 characters. You may need to adjust your printer font size to have the entire title printed on your output. Any title will replace the default title line that is printed when Headings is selected in the Print Selections dialog box.

**Printer Setup.** Click on Printer Setup... to open the Select Printer dialog box, as shown in Figure 6.18, to change print options regarding the type of printer, orientation, paper, and other options. See "Printer Setup" on p. 92 for further details.

**Font.** Click on Font to open the Font dialog box (Figure 6.17) and change the font, font style, or font size for all output except the tree diagram. (To change the font for the tree diagram, use Tree Font.) In order to have more of your output printed on each individual page, you may wish to change the font or font size.

**Figure 6.17 Font dialog box**

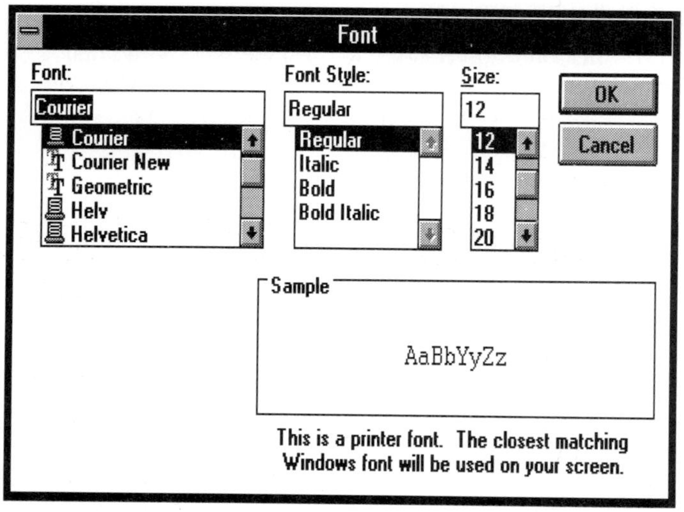


## Printer Setup

This section describes how to control various printer settings, such as page size and orientation. The available options vary for different printers.

To modify printer settings, from the File menu choose

File
 Printer Setup...

This opens the Select Printer dialog box, as shown in Figure 6.18.

**Figure 6.18 Select Printer dialog box**

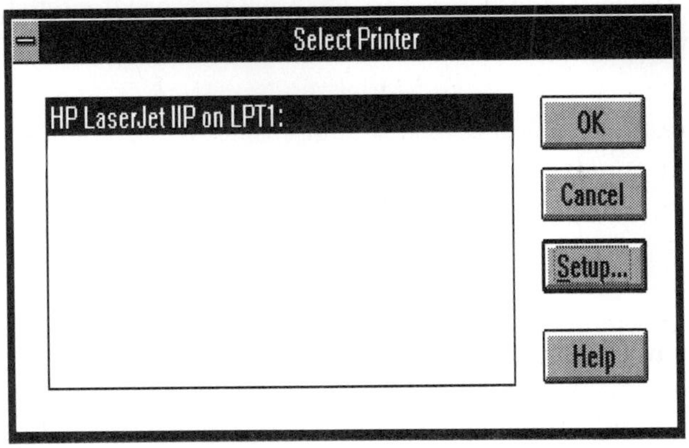


To change the setup of a printer on the list, select the printer and click on Setup.... This opens the Printer Setup dialog box, as shown in Figure 6.19.

**Figure 6.19 Printer Setup dialog box**

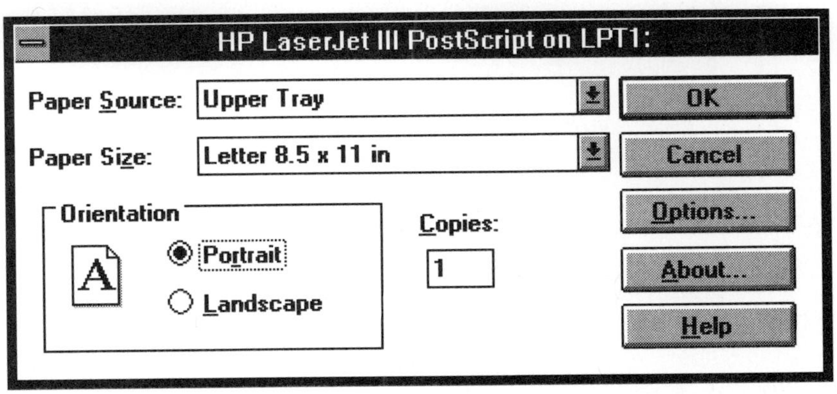


The following are general options that may be changed:

**Orientation**. There are two alternatives:

- **Portrait**. The page is taller than it is wide. This is the default.
- **Landscape**. The page is wider than it is tall.

**Paper Size**. The default is standard letter size (8 1/2 × 11 inches). If you are using a different paper size, such as legal (8 1/2 × 14 inches), change this setting to reflect the new size.

**Copies**. Select the number of copies to print.

**Options**. Click on Options... to set various options regarding the specific type of printer you have selected.

### Exit

To leave the CHAID program, select Exit. When you select Exit, you are asked to confirm the request. This allows you to select No, return to CHAID, and save the tree diagram to an analysis file if you have not done so already.

## Edit Menu

The Edit menu, as shown in Figure 6.20, is used to copy selected output to the clipboard so that it can be pasted into other applications.

**Figure 6.20 Edit menu**

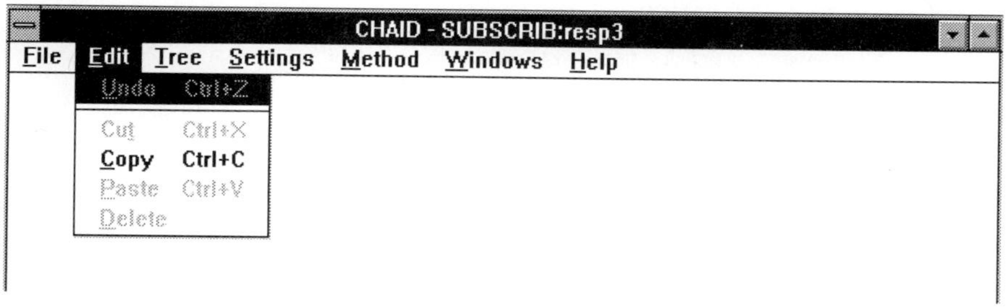


### Copy

To copy output to the clipboard, select Edit Copy to open the Clipboard Selections dialog box. This box is almost identical to the Print Selections box except that there are no Printer Setup, Page Setup, or Font pushbuttons.

After clipping, the output may be pasted into another application, such as a word processor. Use the Paste option to paste the output you've placed in the clipboard. Tree diagrams can have either a "bitmap" or "unformatted text" data type while all other output will have "unformatted text" as their data type.

You may clip five different types of output: tree diagrams, crosstabulations (Tables), documentation, gains charts and predictor significance listings (Predictor). For specific details on the available options, see "Print" on p. 85. For tree diagrams, "bitmap" produces only global tree diagrams in a schematic form that cannot be edited, while "unformatted text" produces a file similar to the *.his* file produced by the original version of CHAID (see Appendix E for further details).

# Tree Menu

The Tree menu is used to develop your tree interactively. Various options lead you through an analysis and allow you to select predictors at each node, automatically grow the tree from a specified node, prune branches from your tree, and rearrange categories of a predictor to suit your needs. The Tree menu is shown in Figure 6.21.

**Figure 6.21 Tree menu**

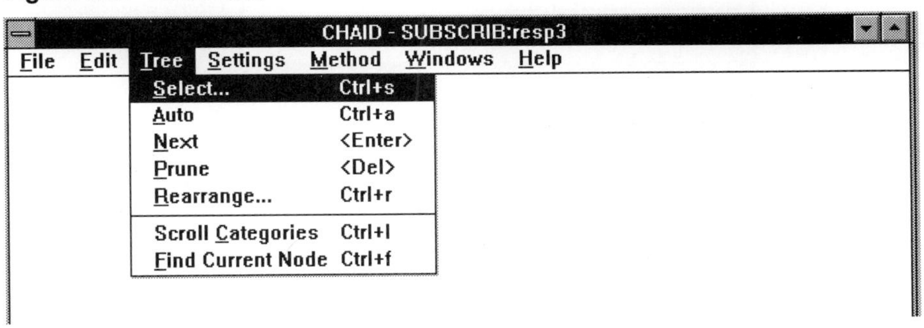


## Select

From the Tree menu, choose Select... to: 1) manually select any predictor to split the current node, 2) display adjusted *p* values, 3) view merged predictor categories, or 4) for SPSS files only, view variable labels. This opens the Select Predictor dialog box, as shown in Figure 6.22. If the current node has not been analyzed previously, CHAID analyzes the node before opening the Select Predictor dialog box.

**Figure 6.22 Select Predictor dialog box**

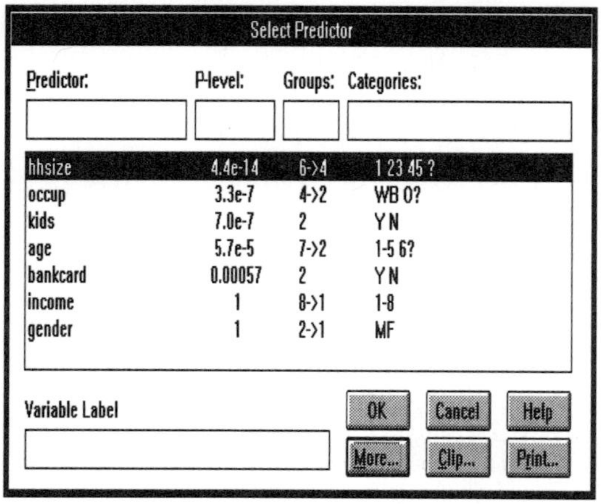


The Select Predictor dialog box contains the predictor's name, *p* value, number of CHAID-defined categories (Groups), and corresponding category symbols (Categories). For example, in Figure 6.22, the variable *hhsize* has six original categories, represented by the symbols 1, 2, 3, 4, 5, and ?.They have been merged into four categories by CHAID (6->4). The CHAID-defined categories are represented by the symbols 1, 23, 45, and ?. The grouping of symbols indicates which categories have been merged. For *hhsize*, categories 2 and 3 have been merged and categories 4 and 5 have been merged.

You may select a predictor by typing its name or highlighting the predictor name on the Predictor list and then clicking on OK, or you may just double-click on a highlighted predictor name. CHAID then recalls the data and splits the node based on the categories of the predictor.

## Predictor Display Options

You can choose the rule for displaying predictors and select the order in which they are displayed. Click on More to open the Predictor Display Options dialog box, as shown in Figure 6.23.

**Figure 6.23 Predictor Display Options dialog box**

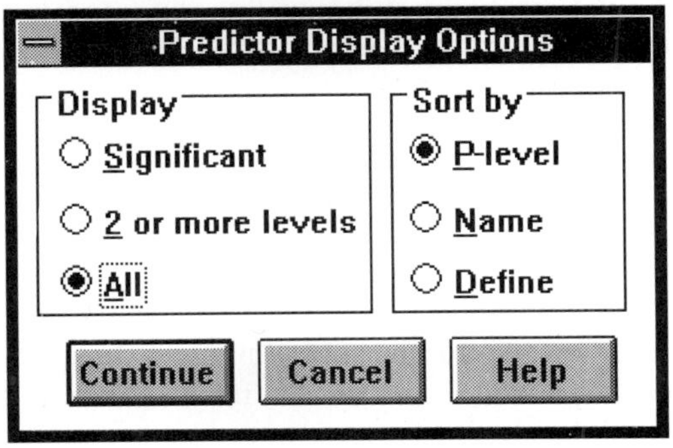


**Display**. To specify which predictors to list, select one of the following alternatives:

- **Significant.** Lists only significant predictors. This is the default.
- **2 or more levels.** Lists only those predictors with two or more categories after category merging.
- **All**. Lists all possible predictors.

**Sort by**.To specify the order in which to list predictors, select one of the following alternatives:

- **P-level**. Sorts predictors in descending order by degree of statistical significance. Statistical significance is measured by the Bonferroni adjusted probability value (*p* value). The lower the *p* value, the more significant the predictor. A *p* value of 0.000000001 is displayed in scientific notation as 1E-9.
- **Name**. Sorts predictors alphabetically by variable name.
- **Define.** Sorts predictors by the order in which variables were read in from the data file.

# Auto

Auto grows the tree automatically from the current node. In auto mode, CHAID chooses the predictor with the lowest *p* value at each level. CHAID stops growing the tree either when there are no more significant predictors to split on or when a user-defined limit is reached. For more information on user-defined limits, see "Options" on p. 102. To interrupt the automatic analysis at any time, press any key.

If you wish to replace the entire contents of your tree with an automatic analysis without recalling your original data file, highlight the root node and select Prune and then Auto from the Tree menu.

Unlike the automatic startup mode setting that may be set under Settings Options, Auto on the Tree menu does not overwrite any preexisting splits but will grow the tree below them. For example, if Auto is selected from the root node and there are already subnodes below, Auto will try to build off of the existing subnodes.

Running Auto from any particular split affects only the nodes below it. If you want to finish growing an entire tree, move to the root node before selecting Auto.

## Next

Next performs the next step that CHAID would carry out in automatic mode for the current node. It is helpful for interactive analysis.

The next step in automatic analysis for the current node is displayed on the message bar at the top of the Global window. (See "Global Window" on p. 115 if the message does not appear.) The message either directs you where to go next in the analysis or suggests what to do next.

If the label <*Analyzed*> is displayed beneath the current node, CHAID displays a message in parentheses at the end of the suggested next step. The message explains why this node was not split.

When the suggested next step is Analyze subgroup and select best predictor, Next performs the analysis and displays the Select Predictor dialog box containing only the current significant predictors sorted by $p$ value (see Figure 6.22). You can select a predictor from the Select Predictor dialog box (see "Select" on p. 95).

## Prune

Prune deletes all nodes directly below the current node. This option allows you to prune the tree, getting rid of any branches that are judged to be extraneous. Move to the node immediately above the predictor that you wish to delete before selecting Prune from the Tree menu. CHAID will delete all splits directly below the current node. If more than one split exists directly under the current node, CHAID requests confirmation with a warning message.

## Rearrange

To rearrange the way in which CHAID combines categories for a predictor or to change the order of the predictor's categories, move to the node above the predictor, and from the menus choose Tree Rearrange. This opens the Rearrange Categories dialog box, as shown in Figure 6.24.

**Figure 6.24 Rearrange Categories dialog box**

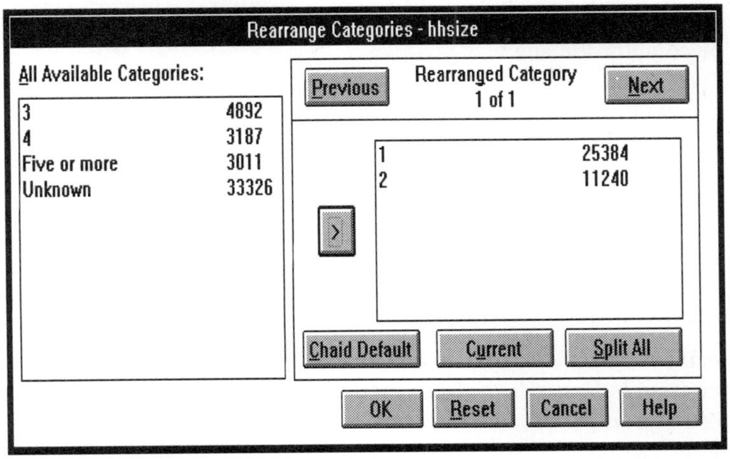


Each original category label for the predictor is displayed in the All Available Categories box along with the number of cases in each category.

To rearrange a predictor:

❶ Highlight a category (or categories) in the All Available Categories box.

❷ Click on the arrow key to move the category (or categories) into the box labeled Rearranged Category 1 of 1. Continue this process for all original categories that you wish to merge together to form new category 1.

❸ When all original categories that you wish to be in new category 1 have been moved, click on Next.

You will now be able to move categories into Rearranged Category 2 of 2. Continue this process for as many new categories as you would like to create. All categories must be selected for inclusion into one (and only one) new category.

❹ Use the Previous and Next pushbuttons to view the current rearrangements. Select OK when completed.

To deselect a category, highlight it in the Rearranged Categories box, and then click on the reverse arrow key.

## Rearranging Monotonic and Floating Variables

CHAID must follow rules regarding predictor combine types while rearranging the categories. If your predictor is monotonic, you can combine only adjacent categories. If your predictor is floating, you can combine only adjacent categories except for the last category, which may be combined with any of the other categories. Only free variables can be combined in any way you like.

When a rule is violated, CHAID displays an error message and stops the operation.

To view the predictor combine type for a predictor, use the Variable Categories option on the Settings menu.

If you want to combine monotonic categories in a nonadjacent way, you must reassign the variable type as Free in the Assign Variables dialog box under File New. For a discussion of predictor combine types, see "Options" on p. 82.

## Keeping Track of Rearranged Variables

The name of any predictor you have rearranged is marked by an asterisk (*) on the tree diagram and in any tables that are produced.

For a rearranged predictor, the *p* value is always the Bonferroni adjusted *p* value reported in the after-merge table. The adjusted *p* value for a rearranged variable is displayed at the bottom of the after-merge row percentage table.

## Reverting, Separating, and Resetting Categories

**CHAID Default.** Click on CHAID Default to revert to the CHAID category arrangement of predictor categories.

**Current.** Click on Current to set the categories to the form they were in before Current Rearrange was selected (the way they last looked on the tree diagram).

**Split All.** Click on Split All to rearrange predictor categories so that each original category is separated from the other categories (that is, there will be one new category for each original before-merge category.) You can also prevent categories of a predictor from combining by setting the eligibility level to be 1.0 under Settings Options.

**Reset.** Click on Reset to start over rearranging. All categories will be listed in the All Available Categories box.

## Scroll Categories

Select Scroll Categories from the Tree menu to scroll through categories of the dependent variable that are not currently visible in the tree nodes. Available only when percentage distribution, not average score, is displayed in the tree nodes. For example, for a two-category dependent variable, CHAID will only display the percentage associated with category 1 of the dependent variable in the tree nodes.

To display the percentage distribution associated with category 2 instead of category 1, select Scroll Categories.

To display more than one percentage in the node at the same time, see the Windows Percents command.

## Find Current Node

If the current node is not visible, this option will locate and highlight the current node in the Local window.

# Settings Menu

The Settings menu, as shown in Figure 6.25, is used to specify various standard and technical options for your analysis and to specify settings for CHAID display colors and default values.

**Figure 6.25 Settings menu**

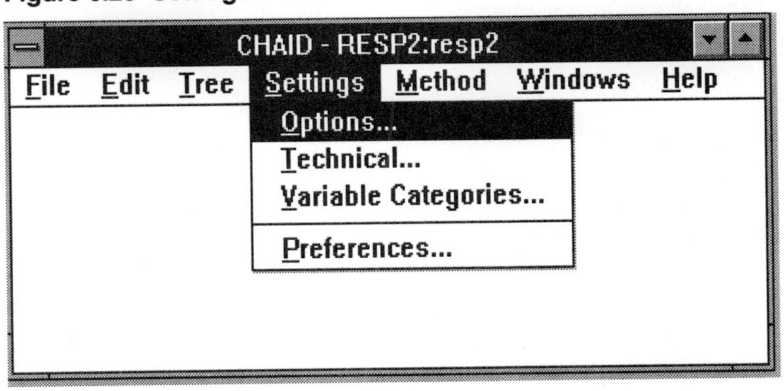

# Options

Select Options... to open the Standard Options dialog box, as shown in Figure 6.26. This box may also be opened by clicking on the Standard... pushbutton in the Assign Variables dialog box under File New.

**Figure 6.26 Standard Options dialog box**

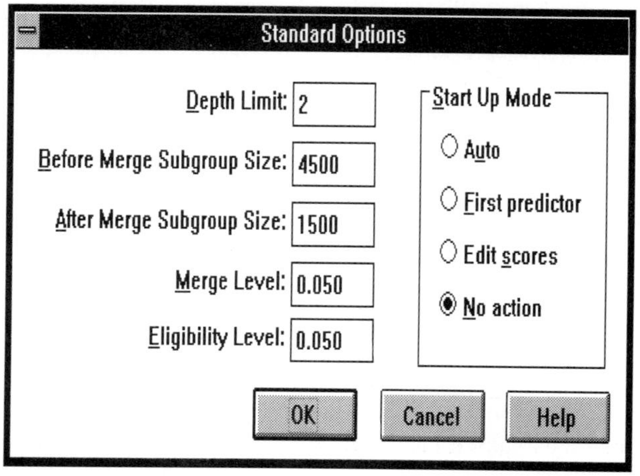


Options displays your current analysis settings. Any change made to these settings will result in a new tree analysis; that is, your current analysis will be erased and you will be placed at the root node of your new analysis.

## Depth Limit

The analysis depth limit is used to limit the size of your tree diagram (that is, how many levels down it goes), when an automatic analysis is performed. By default, the tree diagram is limited to two levels.

A depth limit of two or three is recommended for an initial analysis with a large number of predictors. By limiting analysis to such a depth, the program runs much faster and the results may be used to delete some of the predictors that are not significant during this initial analysis. A second analysis may then be performed with fewer predictors, taking less time than the same analysis with many extraneous predictors.

A depth limit of zero (0) implies no theoretical limit. In practice, CHAID is limited to a maximum depth of 30.

To set the depth limit, type in a value from 0–30.

## Minimum Subgroup Sizes

You can specify both the minimum subgroup size required to allow splitting and the minimum final segment size (terminal node on the tree diagram).

**Before Merge Subgroup Size.** The minimum subgroup size required to allow splitting. The default is 100. The value must be an integer. CHAID does not analyze a subgroup if the (unweighted) sample size falls below the specified value. For example, with the default setting of 100, any subgroup with fewer than 100 observations is not analyzed further and, thus, becomes a terminal node (segment) on the tree diagram.

**After Merge Subgroup Size.** The minimum final segment (terminal node) size. The default value is 50. The value must be an integer. This option insures that final segments contain at least the specified minimum number of observations. For example, with the default setting of 50, all terminal nodes on the tree diagram have at least 50 observations. (For technical details on this option, see Appendix B.)

## Significance Levels

You can specify significance levels for merging or splitting and eligibility.

**Merge Level.** The general level of difficulty for combining categories of a predictor. The default value is 0.05. You can specify a value between 0 and 1. The value is used for all predictors that do not have a specified merge level set under File New. The higher the merge level, the more difficult it is for categories to be combined. If a level of 1.00 is specified, it is likely that no categories will be merged for any predictor. To change the level for some, but not all predictors, use the predictor-specific merge level in the Predictors dialog box (see "Options" on p. 82). Levels assigned in the predictor-specific merge level take precedence over those specified here.

To set a merge level, type in a value from 0–1.00.

**Eligibility Level.** The alpha level (type 1 error rate) for a variable to be considered statistically significant. The default value is 0.05. You can specify a value between 0 and 1. Only predictors having a *p* value less than or equal to alpha are considered to be eligible for splitting subgroups. A *p* value of 0.05 for a predictor means that the observed sample relationship between that predictor and the dependent variable would only occur 5% of the time, if the two variables were, in fact, unrelated in the population. The lower the *p* value, the more statistically significant the relationship.

To change the eligibility level, type in a value from 0–1.00.

## Startup Mode

Select one of the following alternatives to determine the startup mode.

❍ **Auto.** CHAID performs the entire analysis according to your settings and stops when the analysis is complete (or interrupted by clicking on Cancel).

- **First predictor.** CHAID selects the best predictor and completes only the first split of your tree diagram. You can then continue the analysis interactively.
- **Edit scores.** CHAID places you in the Edit Scores dialog box so that you can add or modify scores before beginning your analysis. This option is recommended for ordinal analyses when you wish to alter the default scores for the dependent variable categories.
- **No action.** Only the root node appears with no analysis having taken place. You can then begin the analysis any way you wish. This is the default option.

## Technical

Select Technical... on the Settings menu to open the Technical Options dialog box, as shown in Figure 6.27. This box may also be opened by clicking on the Technical... pushbutton in the Assign Variables dialog box under File New or in the Edit Scores dialog box under Method Nominal or Method Ordinal.

**Figure 6.27 Technical Options dialog box**

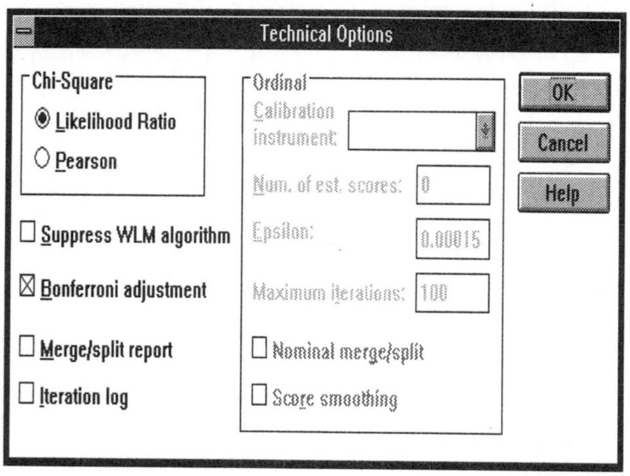


If you already have a tree diagram loaded, changing any one of these settings will restart your analysis from scratch.

**Chi-Square.** Chi-square, applicable to nominal analyses only, offers a choice of the likelihood-ratio chi-square (default) or the Pearson chi-square. Ordinal analyses always use the likelihood-ratio chi-square.

- **Likelihood-ratio.** Chi-square is denoted as *LR chi-square* in the output.
- **Pearson.** Pearson chi-square is denoted as *chi-square* in the output. (The original release of SPSS/PC+ CHAID used Pearson chi-square.)

- **Suppress WLM algorithm.** This option allows you to use or not to use the weighted loglinear modeling (WLM) algorithm for the computation of chi-square statistics associated with each predictor. It is applicable only if a weight variable is designated. If no weights are specified, the WLM algorithm is not used. In the case that the weights assigned by a weight variable are a function of the dependent variable, the WLM algorithm may be turned off without affecting the statistics, and will speed up the processing. For example, in the case of a dichotomous dependent variable, where the weight variable is 1 for all observations in category 1 and, say, 100 for all observations in category 2, WLM may be turned off. In other cases where complex sampling weights are employed, the WLM algorithm should be used to ensure that the analysis is performed correctly. (For technical details on the WLM algorithm, see Appendix B.)
- **Bonferroni adjustment.** Used to apply the Bonferroni adjustment. The Bonferroni adjustment is used in the calculation of the *p* value for each predictor in order to take into account the fact that some categories of the predictor were merged together. The amount of the adjustment depends upon the predictor type (free, monotonic, or float). In general, we recommend using the Bonferroni adjustment.
- **Merge/split report.** Merge/split report produces a report containing technical information on category merging and will appear as part of a file saved with the analysis run name and a *.log* extension, such as *resp2.log*. This report is for technical users and can be printed outside the CHAID program. This option should not be used in conjunction with Iteration log (See below).
- **Iteration log.** Iteration log produces a report containing technical information on the iterations and will appear as part of a file saved with the analysis run name and a *.log* extension, such as *resp2.log*. This report is for technical users and can be printed outside the CHAID program. This option should not be used in conjunction with Merge/split report (See above).

## Ordinal Analysis Options

**Calibration instrument.** Calibration instrument, applicable only under ordinal analyses, is used to manually designate that predictor variable as the instrument to estimate one or more dependent variable scores. The degrees of freedom used in the computation of the *p* value of this predictor will be adjusted according to the number of "estimated" scores.

The instrument variable is initialized and reset to `none` each time you begin a new analysis. When you request CHAID to estimate dependent variable scores by setting some scores to `e` or through the use of the Calibration option, CHAID sets the instrument to the predictor that you chose in the Select Instrument dialog box.

Select this option to specify the instrument when CHAID does not know (or no longer knows) that you used a predictor to obtain one or more dependent variable category scores. Use the Num. of est. scores option to specify how many scores were estimated based on this instrument.

**Num. of est. scores.** Num. of est. scores, applicable only under ordinal analyses, is used to adjust the number of degrees of freedom (df) associated with that predictor that you selected to be the "instrument" when one or more dependent variable scores are estimated. This option affects the calculation of the $p$ value for testing the significance of the instrument, as estimated for ordinal analyses:

$$DF = I - 1 + \min(J - 2, N)$$

where $I$ = number of categories for the predictor (instrument), $J$ = number of categories for the dependent variable, and $N$ = number of estimated scores.

For all predictors other than the instrument, $N$=0. For the predictor used as the instrument, $N$, by default, equals the number of categories assigned an `e` score, or $J$ if the calibration option is employed to estimate scores for all categories.

$N$=0 initially and is reset to 0 each time the nominal or ordinal method is selected to begin a new analysis.

**Epsilon**. Applicable only under the ordinal method. Convergence is achieved if certain parameter values are all found to be within epsilon of their theoretical maximum-likelihood values after performing at most the maximum iterations. Epsilon must be a positive number.

To change the epsilon setting, type in the epsilon number you want. For example, type `IE-8` or `1e-8` for 0.00000001.

Epsilon is used in conjunction with the Maximum iterations option to determine how many iterations are performed under the ordinal method algorithm.

**Maximum iterations**. Applicable only under the ordinal method.

If convergence is not achieved to the prespecified epsilon level after performing the maximum iterations, CHAID displays an Ordinal Warning message.

Decreasing the value of maximum iterations may speed up the ordinal analysis at the cost of providing more approximate results and more Ordinal Warning messages.

For information regarding how to handle Ordinal Warning messages, see "Epsilon, Iterations, and Achieving Convergence" on p. 114.

**Nominal merge/split.** Nominal merge/split, applicable only under the ordinal method, changes the method of merging categories to that employed under the nominal method but leaves all other statistics unaffected.

This option may be employed to approximate the ordinal category-merging process when the full ordinal algorithm takes too long to perform.

**Score smoothing.** Score smoothing, applicable only to ordinal analyses, is used to implement smoothing of estimated scores.

If the estimates from a calibration would produce scores that are not ordered from high to low or vice versa, score smoothing will cause some categories of the dependent variable to be merged until the category scores are ordered.

Use Score smoothing when the specific category scores are not known (and will be estimated by Calibration), but it is known that the current category ordering is such that the scores should go from high to low or low to high.

After new scores appear, you may use the Scale option to change scores in descending order to ascending order or vice versa.

## Variable Categories

Select Variable Categories... to open the Variable Categories dialog box, as shown in Figure 6.28, to display the full category symbols and labels for the predictor directly below the currently highlighted node along with the predictor combine type (monotonic, free, or float) and frequency counts (both before and after merging).

**Figure 6.28 Variable Categories dialog box**

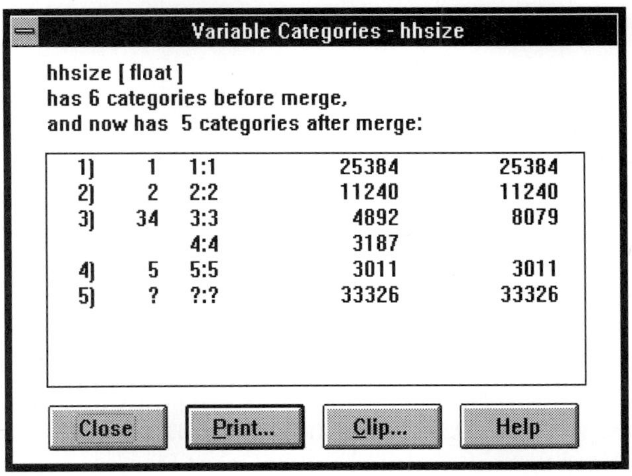

## Preferences

Select Preferences... to open the Preferences dialog box, as shown in Figure 6.29, which allows you to set CHAID display colors and default values.

**Figure 6.29 Preferences dialog box**

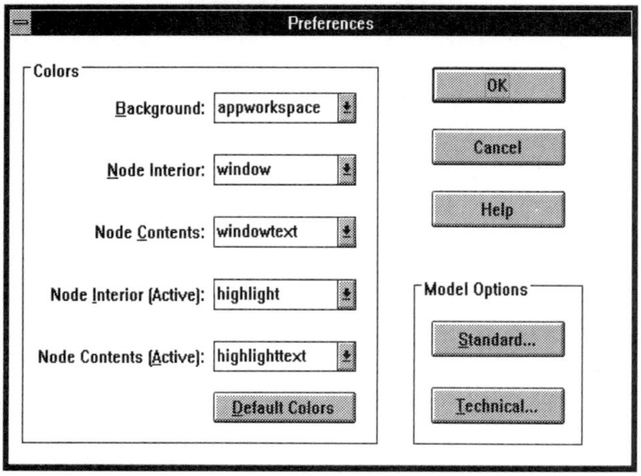


**Colors**. You may adjust colors for the background, node interior, and node contents for either all nodes or the currently highlighted node (Active).

The custom option allows you to select custom colors from a color palette. All other options refer to current screen colors.

Select Default Colors in order to restore colors to their original settings.

**Model Options**. Select Standard... or Technical... to change various default options for all future CHAID analyses. For example, if you select Standard and change the Depth Limit to 4, all future analyses begun with File New will have a default Depth Limit value of 4. For more information regarding the options that may be changed, see "Options" on p. 102 and "Technical" on p. 104.

# Method Menu

The Method menu is used to determine whether the dependent variable will be treated as nominal or ordinal for statistical computations. If the dependent variable has only two categories, the statistical computations under these methods are identical. The Method menu is shown in Figure 6.30. A check mark signifies the method currently in use.

**Figure 6.30 Method menu**

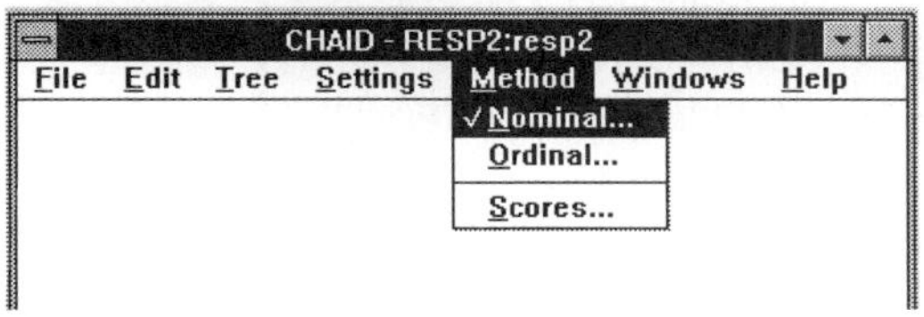


The selection of either Nominal or Ordinal begins a new CHAID analysis. Thus, several different analyses of a designated dependent variable may be performed without exiting from the program. For example, an analysis using the nominal method could be followed by several different ordinal analyses, each based on different category scores. Scores can also be used to delete or merge selected dependent variable categories in an analysis.

Selection of any of the Method options opens the Edit Scores dialog box, as shown in Figure 6.31.

## Nominal

Nominal performs nominal analyses, where no scores or values are used by the CHAID algorithm in the computation of $p$ values. It is the default method for CHAID.

If you currently have a CHAID analysis on your screen, you are asked whether it is OK to erase the tree. Select Yes to continue. The Edit Scores dialog box opens, as shown in Figure 6.31.

**Figure 6.31 Edit Scores dialog box**

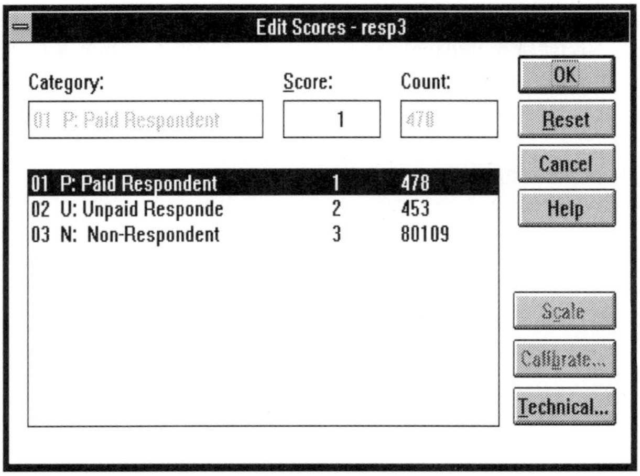


The Edit Scores dialog box contains the sequential category numbers, symbols, labels, and scores for each category of the dependent variable, as well as the counts (or weighted counts) of observations that fall into these categories.

To begin a nominal analysis, just click on OK since nominal analyses do not require category scores. However, scores assigned in this dialog box will override any default or user-defined scores. You can specify two or more categories of the dependent variable to be merged by assigning the same score to these categories, or you can delete from the analysis all observations falling into a dependent variable category by entering a period (.) as the score for that category. For example, after developing a CHAID segmentation based on a three-category nominal dependent variable, select Nominal once again and assign the scores 100, 0, 0 to develop an alternative segmentation of the two-category dependent variable (categories 2 and 3 will be merged, since they have the same score).

You can use scores to rearrange the order of categories of the dependent variable. For example, if your dependent variable was *region*—Northeast (NE), South (S), Midwest (MW), Southeast (SE) and Pacific (P), for a particular purpose you may wish to have S and SE appear next to each other in the output for easier analysis. Assigning the scores 1, 2, 3, 4, 5 and then selecting order from high to low would allow you to rearrange the way in which the categories are shown. Rearranging the order of categories of a nominal dependent variable will not affect the analysis in any way. It will only affect the display order for categories of the dependent variable on the tree diagram and in tables. Also be careful as gains charts will use these scores instead of the default scores (see “Gain Scores” on p. 122 for more information regarding gains scores).

Click on Technical... to open the Technical Options dialog box and change various options such as Chi-square, Suppress WLM algorithm, Bonferroni adjustment, Merge/split report and Iteration log. For more information on these options, see "Technical" on p. 104.

## Ordinal

Ordinal performs ordinal analyses. The ordinal method should be used for all dependent variables that have ordered categories. CHAID will attempt to find (good) segments that have high average scores and (bad) segments that have low average scores.

Category scores are used in the computation of predictor *p* values to provide more powerful tests of predictor significance. Category scores are required and can either be preset from numeric codes in your data file, preset by selecting Edit Scores as your startup mode under File New, or entered directly through the Edit Scores dialog box. If needed, CHAID can also estimate one or more (or all) of the scores.

If you currently have a CHAID analysis on your screen, you are asked whether it is OK to erase the tree before beginning a new analysis. Select Yes to continue. The Edit Scores dialog box opens, as shown in Figure 6.31. You can modify the current category scores either by entering new scores directly or through the use of one of the scaling or estimation options.

### Assigning Scores

To assign a new score for a category:

1. Highlight a category of the dependent variable.
2. Double-click the mouse.
3. Type in the new score.
4. Click the mouse to set the score.
5. Click on OK when all scores have been entered.

### Score Ordering

CHAID will alert you if the scores that you have assigned are not ordered from high-to-low or low-to-high by opening the Score Order dialog box, as shown in Figure 6.32. Note that the order of the categories has no effect upon the analysis.

**Figure 6.32 Score Order dialog box**

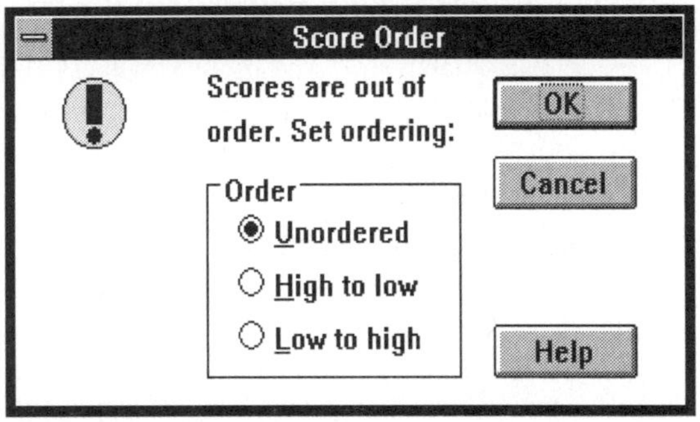


In the Order group, select one of the following alternatives:

- **Unordered**. Leaves categories in their current order.
- **High to low**. Changes the ordering in which to dependent variable categories are displayed so that they are ordered from high to low.
- **Low to high**. Changes the ordering in which to dependent variable categories are displayed so that they are ordered from low to high.

Selection of any of these options affects only the order in which the dependent variable categories are displayed.

## Special Score Characters

Assigning the period (.) as a score will cause CHAID to omit from the analysis all observations that fall into the particular category of a dependent variable. If you choose to delete a responder category, check to make sure that your settings for minimum subgroup size (before and after) are still valid for the number of cases that remain.

Assigning the special character `e` or `E` as a score will cause CHAID to estimate the score for that category. This option is available only for ordinal analyses. If an `e` or `E` is entered as a score, CHAID will prompt you to designate a predictor to be used as an instrument to estimate the score. You should select one of the predictors that you believe to be associated with the dependent variable as the instrument.

If you wish to estimate some but not all scores, you must assign numeric scores to at least two categories of the dependent variable. If you assign an `e` score to too many categories, CHAID will display the message At least 2 scores must be fixed. If you receive this message, you must replace some of the `e` scores with numeric scores to continue. For further information on the estimation of scores, see Appendix B. If you wish to estimate all scores (or all scores other than those assigned a period), use the Calibrate option, which is discussed below.

## Calibrating, Scaling, and Resetting Scores

Click on Calibrate to open the Select Instrument to Calibrate dialog box, as shown in Figure 6.33, which is used to produce maximum likelihood score estimates for each category you assigned an e, or all categories if you haven't assigned any e scores.

**Figure 6.33 Select Instrument to Calibrate dialog box**

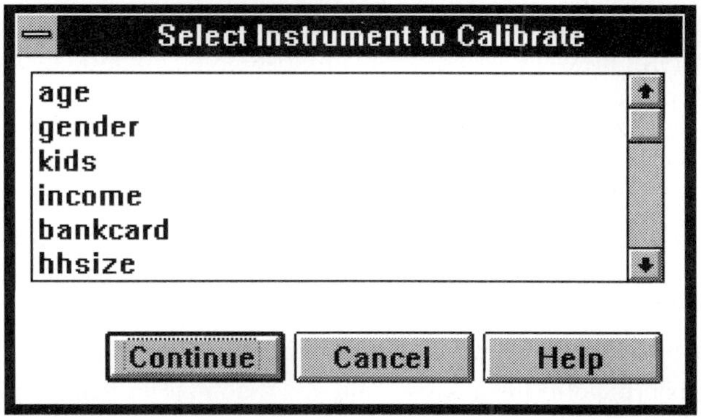


Upon opening the Select Instrument to Calibrate dialog box, a list of the predictor variables will appear. Select the predictor you believe to be associated with the dependent variable. If after selecting a predictor CHAID displays the message This predictor is not an eligible instrument, you must select a different predictor. A predictor is not eligible to be used as an instrument if there are more than (I – 2)*( J – 2) empty cells (that is, zero observed counts) in the I × J table of the predictor by dependent variable. If no predictors are eligible, you cannot estimate scores for the dependent variable. (To return to your analysis, you may need to replace the e scores with numeric scores.) For more information on calibration and the requirements for a predictor to be used as the instrument, see Appendix B.

- Click on Scale to apply a linear transformation to scores so that the highest score becomes 100 and the lowest becomes 0. If Scale is applied a second time (or if the original scores already range between 0 and 100), the high and low scores are reversed by applying the transformation NEW = 100 – OLD.
- Click on Reset to reset scores to their original values, that is, to the values in your original data file, or, if scores were not included in the data file, to the values initially assigned by CHAID, beginning with 1 for the first category. You can select Reset to separate categories you have merged or deleted using the special score characters in earlier analyses.
- Click on Technical to open the Technical Options dialog box and change various ordinal analysis options. For more information on these options, see "Technical" on p. 104.

### Epsilon, Iterations, and Achieving Convergence

The ordinal method employs an iterative maximum likelihood algorithm in the computation of the statistical significance ($p$ value) for each predictor. To be certain that the correct chi-square value is obtained, enough iterations need to be performed so that the algorithm converges. (Convergence is achieved when successive iterations cause certain parameters to be within epsilon of the maximum-likelihood estimate.) If convergence is not achieved to the prespecified epsilon level after performing the specified number of iterations, a warning message will appear. In most cases, click on Close and continue your analysis as planned.

### Improving Precision

You may change the settings for either epsilon or maximum iterations. In general, a higher value for epsilon and a lower value for iterations will speed up the analyses of the best predictor. However, if the algorithm does not converge, the selection of the best predictor and associated $p$ values may not be correct.

1. If the predictor is critical to the analysis and $d$ is much larger than epsilon (the default for epsilon is 0.00015), you may wish to use the Tree Prune option to undo the current split. Then increase the number of iterations and reanalyze.
2. If the predictor is critical to the analysis and $c2 > c1$, perform action in step 1 above unless $i <$ iteration max; then, decrease epsilon.

The values for maximum iterations and epsilon may be changed during an analysis using the Technical option on the Settings menu (see "Technical" on p. 104).

Sometimes in a large analysis, you may receive many ordinal warning messages. To bypass these messages, you may select Tree Auto to grow the tree and one warning message will be produced at the end of the analysis.

## Scores

Used to view the current scores without restarting a new analysis.

# Windows Menu

Use the windows menu, as shown in Figure 6.34, to specify options regarding the display of the tree diagram and other output on the screen. There are four types of output windows: Global window, Local window, Table window, and Gains Chart window.

**Figure 6.34 Windows menu**

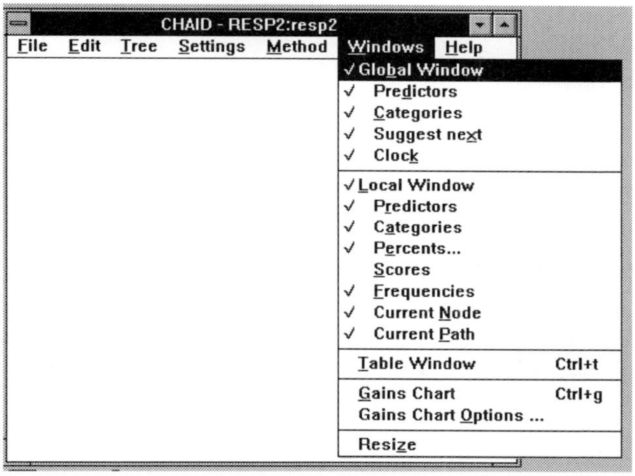


Check marks next to an option signify that it is in use.

## Global Window

The Global window contains the Global tree diagram. The Global window shows a much larger portion of the tree diagram than the Local window, since the tree nodes have been reduced in size.

The following options pertain to the Global window:

**Predictors**. Used to show predictor names in the global window tree diagram.

**Categories**. Used to show category names in global window tree diagram.

**Suggest next**. A message bar, which details the next step CHAID would take if it was running under automatic mode, will appear at the top of the Global window. To perform the suggested next step, just press enter or select Tree Next.

**Clock**. A clock will appear in the upper right corner of the Global window.

## Local Window

The Local window is used to view one parent node and up to five child nodes or subnodes at one time. The nodes of the tree diagram in the Local window contain more detailed information than the nodes in the Global window. For information on how to interpret a tree diagram, see "A Tree Diagram" on p. 4.

The following options pertain to the Local window:

**Predictors**. Used to show predictor names in local window tree diagram

**Categories**. Used to show category names in the local window tree diagram.

**Percents...**. Selecting Percents... opens the Select Categories to Show dialog box, as shown in Figure 6.35. Select those categories of the dependent variable for which percentages are to be displayed. A list of all categories of the dependent variable will appear.

**Figure 6.35 Select Categories to Show dialog box**

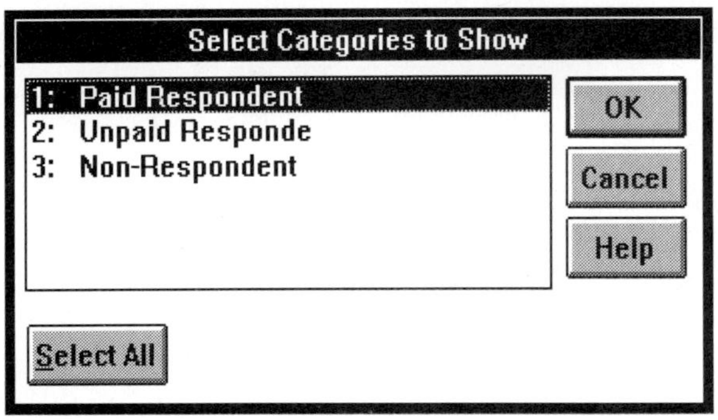


Highlight those categories you wish to appear in the nodes of the tree diagram. Then select OK. If you choose not to show all categories in your tree nodes, you may still use the Tree Scroll Categories option to scroll through the other categories.

Use Select All to have all the categories of the dependent variable appear in the tree nodes.

**Scores**. Used to display the average dependent variable score in the tree nodes. Default when the ordinal method is in use.

**Frequencies**. Used to show the number of observations in the current subgroup. Preceded by n=.

**Current Node**. If you select Current Node, a box that provides information regarding the current node will appear in the upper right corner of your Local window. Current node information includes variable name, depth level and which category you are currently on (for example, 2/5 is equal to being on category 2 of 5 for a particular variable).

**Current Path.** If you select Current Path, a box that gives a more detailed description than Current Node of where you are currently located on the tree diagram will appear in the upper left corner of your Local window. Current path information includes your full path and what exists at the next level below the current node.

## Table Window

Used to produce crosstabulations of the current predictor (rows) by the dependent variable (columns). (See Figure 6.36.) The table will be automatically updated as options are changed. You may double-click on any highlighted node that has a predictor below it to bring up the Table window. This is an easy way to bring up the Table window if it is hidden behind other windows. If a weight variable is in use, frequency counts in the table may differ from total counts due to rounding.

If the message Table Data Not Available appears in the Table window, there is either no subnode under the currently highlighted node or CHAID needs to recalculate the table. To recalculate the table, just click on the tree node.

Options for the Table window are at the bottom of the Table window and include before or after category merging and row, column, or total percentages or frequency counts.

**Figure 6.36 Table window**

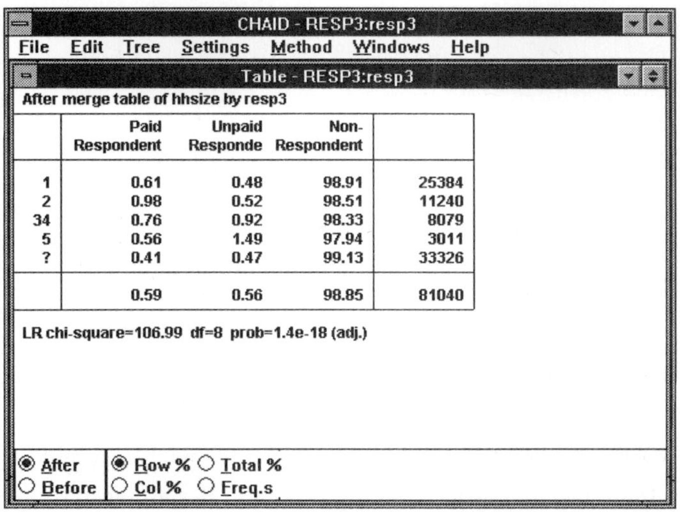


To specify the category merging status of the predictor variable, select one of the following alternatives:

❍ **Before.** Uses the original categories of the predictor variable, not the merged CHAID categories, in the crosstabulation. Category labels will be used in the table.

- **After**. Uses the merged categories of the predictor variable produced by CHAID in the crosstabulation. This is the default. Category symbols will be used in the table. If no categories were merged by CHAID, this option will produce the same tables as the Before option.

To specify the type of percentage or a frequency count for the table cell contents, select one of the following alternatives:

- **Row %.** Table entries for each row will be the conditional percentage distribution of the dependent variable. The percentage within each row sums to 100%. If Ordinal is selected on the Method menu, the last column of the table contains the average score and the individual dependent variable category scores appear at the bottom of the table in a row, as shown in Figure 6.37.

**Figure 6.37 Percentage scores in Table window**

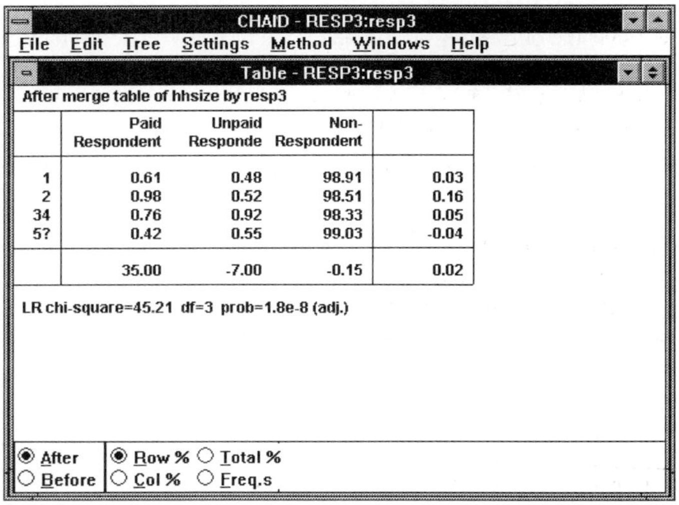


- **Col %**. Table entries for each column will be the percentage distribution of the predictor. The percentage within each column sums to 100%.
- **Total %**. Table entries will be the percentage of the total subgroup.
- **Freq.s**. Table entries will be frequency counts. If a weight variable is used, the crosstabulations are based on weighted counts. The weighted counts are rounded to integers in the display.

At the bottom of the table, CHAID provides the chi-square test for independence (when using the nominal method) or the test for nonassociation (when using the ordinal method), as well as the associated number of degrees of freedom (df) and probability values (prob). By default, the chi-square value is the likelihood-ratio (LR) chi-square, which is recommended. When using the nominal method, you may optionally obtain the Pearson chi-square (see "Technical" on p. 104). The *p* value displayed is the Bonferroni adjusted *p* value. See Appendix B for an explanation of *p* values. For more information regarding the interpretation of tables, see "Crosstabulations" on p. 21 in Chapter 3.

## Gains Chart and Gains Chart Options

Selecting Gains Chart opens the Gains dialog box, which displays detail or summary gains charts for your current tree diagram. (See "Crosstabulations" on p. 21 in Chapter 3 for details on how to read and interpret the gains charts.) Selecting Gains Chart Options... opens the Gains Chart Options dialog box, as shown in Figure 6.38, where you may specify the type of gains chart that will appear in the Gains dialog box.

**Figure 6.38 Gains Chart Options dialog box**

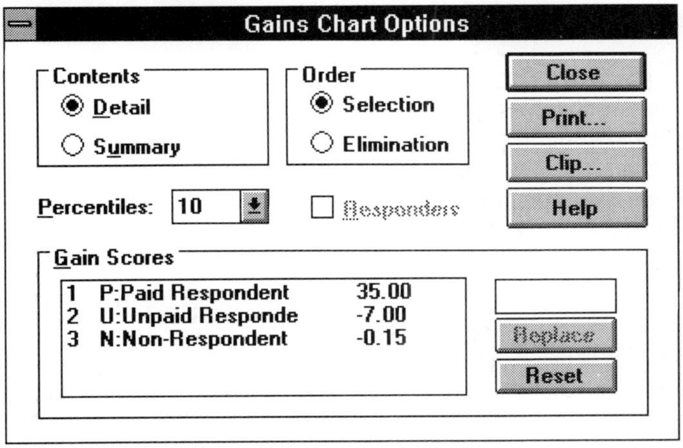


- For the Nominal analysis method, the default gains charts are based on the percentage in the first category of the dependent variable.
- For the Ordinal analysis method, the default gains charts are based on the average category scores where the category scores are the same as those used in the ordinal analysis.
- The default gains charts are overridden if user-defined scores are assigned or the Gain Scores option is used.

## Contents

Choose one of the following alternatives to produce either detail or summary gains charts in the Gains window:

❍ **Detail.** Detail produces a detail gains chart. A detail gains chart contains a row for each terminal node, or segment, of the tree diagram, and rank orders all of the segments from best to worst (or worst to best).

**Figure 6.39 Detail gains chart**

Gains - RESP3:resp3

| Id | size | % of all | score | index | Cum: size | % of all | score | index |
|---|---|---|---|---|---|---|---|---|
| 2 | 11,240 | 13.9 | 0.98 | 166 | 11,240 | 13.9 | 0.98 | 166 |
| 3 | 8,079 | 10.0 | 0.76 | 128 | 19,319 | 23.8 | 0.89 | 150 |
| 1 | 25,384 | 31.3 | 0.61 | 104 | 44,703 | 55.2 | 0.73 | 124 |
| 4 | 3,011 | 3.7 | 0.56 | 96 | 47,714 | 58.9 | 0.72 | 122 |
| 5 | 33,326 | 41.1 | 0.41 | 69 | 81,040 | 100.0 | 0.59 | 100 |

The detail gains chart in Figure 6.39 contains an ID number that corresponds to a segment (terminal node) on the tree diagram. Individual and cumulative information is provided for the segment size, percentage of total sample, average score, and index. The index for a given segment measures the average response score for that segment relative to the average score for the total sample. For example, in Figure 6.39, segment 2 has an index of 128 (that is, .76/.59=128 , where .59% is the overall response rate for this sample.)

The index is not meaningful when the average score for the entire sample is less than or equal to 0 and is displayed as 0 for all segments in this case.

For nominal dependent variables, by default a score of 100 is used for the first category and 0 for all other categories. Hence, the score column in a detail chart reflects the percentage distribution for category 1 of the dependent variable. For example, when category 1 represents response as in Figure 6.39, the score for each segment represents a response rate; segment 2 has a response rate of 2.39%, segment 4 has a response rate of 1.92%, and these two segments combined have a cumulative response rate of 2.02%.

For detailed gains charts, the path (the list of predictors and their categories used to construct this segment) of any particular highlighted segment (row) is displayed in the Path box. To open the Path box for any particular segment, click on the segment. Click on Goto to make the currently highlighted segment the current node when you return to the tree windows.

❍ **Summary**. Summary produces a summary gains chart. To view the summary gains chart, as shown in Figure 6.40, select Summary in the Gains Chart Options dialog box and then select Gains Charts from the Windows menu. The summary chart, also referred to as the quantile gains chart, displays cumulative results at fixed percentage points of the running segment size total. It describes the results that would have been obtained based on the percentage of cases having the highest (or lowest) average score. For example, in Figure 6.40, the highest responding 40% of the households who were mailed the subscription offer responded at a rate of .77%, for an index of 131, or 31% higher than the average household.

**Figure 6.40 Summary gains chart**

Gains - RESP3:resp3

| tile | size | score | index |
|---|---|---|---|
| 10 | 8,104 | 0.98 | 166 |
| 20 | 16,208 | 0.91 | 154 |
| 30 | 24,312 | 0.83 | 141 |
| 40 | 32,416 | 0.77 | 131 |
| 50 | 40,520 | 0.74 | 126 |
| 60 | 48,624 | 0.71 | 121 |
| 70 | 56,728 | 0.67 | 113 |
| 80 | 64,832 | 0.64 | 108 |
| 90 | 72,936 | 0.61 | 103 |
| 100 | 81,040 | 0.59 | 100 |

The summary chart contains the quantile groupings ("tile"), cumulative segment size ("size"), cumulative average score ("score"), and a cumulative index, calculated as the average response score for that quantile relative to the average score for the entire sample. If the average score for the entire sample is less than or equal to 0, the index is not meaningful. In this case, 0 is displayed for all segments.

For nominal dependent variables, by default a score of 100 is used for the first category and 0 for all other categories. Hence, the score column on a summary chart reflects the percent distribution for category 1 of the dependent variable.

## Additional Options

The following additional options are available:

- **Percentiles**. Select Percentiles to specify the percentile interval for quantiles for the summary gains chart. By default, segments are grouped into 10 quantiles at 10% intervals. You may select an alternative number of quantiles for the summary gains chart to display (1%, 2%, 5%, 10%, 20% or 25%). For example, selecting 25% will produce a summary gains chart with 4 quantiles at 25% intervals.
- **Responders.** This option is available for charts when one category (or categories) of the dependent variable is singled out as the "response" category (categories) and is assigned a score(s) of 100, while all other categories are assigned a score of 0. A "resp" (the number of responders in this segment or quantile) column and "%resp" (percentage of the total responses in this segment or quantile) column will be displayed in your charts. For detail charts, both individual and cumulative totals will be displayed.

**Figure 6.41 Summary gains chart with responder option**

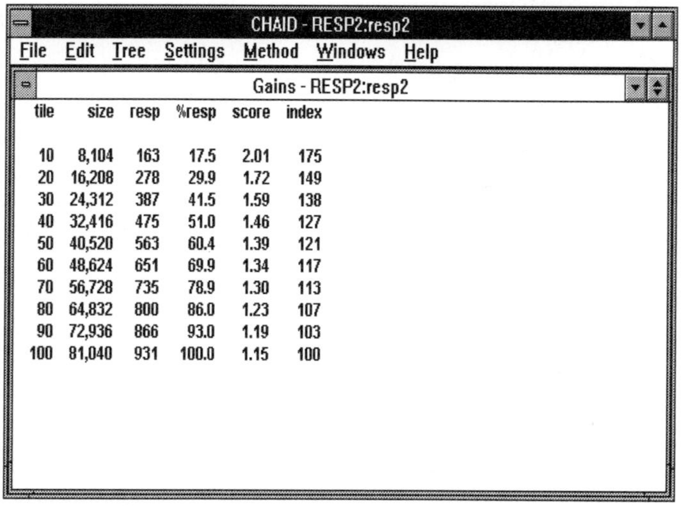


| tile | size | resp | %resp | score | index |
|---|---|---|---|---|---|
| 10 | 8,104 | 163 | 17.5 | 2.01 | 175 |
| 20 | 16,208 | 278 | 29.9 | 1.72 | 149 |
| 30 | 24,312 | 387 | 41.5 | 1.59 | 138 |
| 40 | 32,416 | 475 | 51.0 | 1.46 | 127 |
| 50 | 40,520 | 563 | 60.4 | 1.39 | 121 |
| 60 | 48,624 | 651 | 69.9 | 1.34 | 117 |
| 70 | 56,728 | 735 | 78.9 | 1.30 | 113 |
| 80 | 64,832 | 800 | 86.0 | 1.23 | 107 |
| 90 | 72,936 | 866 | 93.0 | 1.19 | 103 |
| 100 | 81,040 | 931 | 100.0 | 1.15 | 100 |

## Order

Choose one of the following alternatives from the Order group:.

- ❍ **Selection.** A selection report ranks segments from high to low. The dependent category percentage is sorted in descending order, and the cumulative statistics reflect the successive addition of each new segment.
- ❍ **Elimination.** An elimination report ranks segments from low to high. The dependent category percentage is sorted in ascending order, and the cumulative statistics reflect the successive elimination of segments.

## Gain Scores

Gain Scores produces gains charts based on average scores for each category of the dependent variable. Scores entered on this form are used only for the gains charts and not in conducting the actual analysis. Changing scores within the Gains Chart dialog box does not change your current analysis other than to recalculate the average score for each node based on the new scores. To actually run an analysis based on the new scores, you would need to change the scores using the Ordinal option on the Method menu.

- ❍ **Default scores.** When the nominal method is in use, the default scores are 100 for the first category and 0 for all others; thus, the gains chart will be based on the percentage falling into the first category of the dependent variable. When the ordinal method is in use, the defaults are any scores that are on the original data file; if none exist, CHAID assigns scores of 1, 2, 3, etc., in the order in which the categories are read. Always verify the scores in the Gains Chart dialog box before producing your gains charts.

❍ **User-defined scores.** To modify a score, highlight a category by clicking on it, type in the new score in the box above the Replace button, and then click on Replace to replace the old score. Note that the special character scores (.) and (e), which can be used when entering scores from the Method menu, cannot be used here.

- Click on Reset to set scores used in calculating the gains charts to their original values.
- Click on Print to open the print selections box to print gains charts (or any form of output).
- To print a gains chart, in the Print Selections dialog box, click on Gains chart and then specify which reports you want printed in the Gains Chart dialog box. The defaults are a detail selection report plus a segment index report. For more information on the Print Selections dialog box, see "Print" on p. 85.

Subsequent scores set under the nominal or ordinal method will overwrite any scores that you assign here.

## Resize

Use this command to adjust the global and local tree windows so that all frames are visible.

# Appendix A
# The CHAID Algorithm

This appendix describes the segmentation algorithm used in CHAID. The algorithm has three stages: merging, splitting, and stopping.

## Stage 1: Merging

For each predictor, $x_1, x_2, \ldots, x_k$, CHAID merges nonsignificant categories by following these steps:

1. Form a full two-way crosstabulation with the dependent variable.
2. For each pair of categories that is eligible to be merged, compute chi-square statistics (pairwise chi-squares) to test for independence between the pair of categories and the dependent variable (all categories of the dependent variable are used). If the ordinal method is selected, the procedure described in "Probabilities for Ordinal Dependent Variables" on p. 129 in Appendix B is used to compute pairwise chi-squares.
3. Compute the $p$ value for each pairwise chi-square. If any pairs are nonsignificant, merge the pair having the lowest chi-square value into a single joint category, and go to step 4. If all remaining pairs are significant, go to step 5. (To change the default significance level, 0.05, for all predictors, see "Options" on p. 102. To change predictor-specific merge levels, see "Change Merge Level. The user can control the level of difficulty of combining categories for a specific predictor by specifying a predictor-specific merge level. The higher the level, the more difficult it will be for categories of this predictor to be combined. If a level of 1.00 is specified, no categories will be merged for that predictor." on p. 83.)
4. For any joint category containing three or more categories, test to see if any predictor category should be unmerged using the significance level of the chi-square statistic that compares the category with the others in the joint category. If the chi-square is significant, split the category from the others. If more than one category is eligible to be split, split the one having the largest chi-square. Return to step 3.
5. Merge any category having fewer observations than the specification for the minimum subgroup size (after split) with the most similar other category, as measured by the smallest pairwise chi-square.
6. Compute the Bonferroni adjusted $p$ value for the merged categories.

## Stage 2: Splitting

For predictors with a statistically significant adjusted *p* value, split the group on the predictor having the lowest *p* value. Each of the merged categories of the predictor becomes a new subgroup of the parent group. If no predictor has a significant *p* value, do not split the group. (To change the default significance level, 0.05, see "Options" on p. 102.)

## Stage 3: Stopping

Return to step 1 to analyze the next subgroup that contains at least as many observations as the specification for the minimum size of the subgroup (before the split). Stop when all subgroups have been analyzed or when they contain too few cases.

# Appendix B
# Probability Values

The **probability value** (*p* value) used in CHAID is the probability that the observed relationship between the predictor and the dependent variable would occur if the predictor and the dependent variable were statistically independent. The relationship is judged to be statistically significant if the *p* value is less than or equal to the significance level technical parameter (alpha). The "best" predictor is the one that has the lowest *p* value that is less than or equal to alpha.

The estimation of the *p* value depends on whether the nominal or ordinal method of analysis is used. If the ordinal method is selected, the *p* value is based on a special test of nonindependence called the **Y association** (see "Probabilities for Ordinal Dependent Variables" on p. 129). If the nominal method is selected, CHAID tests for any type of nonindependence (see "Probabilities for Nominal Dependent Variables" on p. 127).

For any predictor, CHAID computes an unadjusted *p* value and a Bonferroni adjusted *p* value before predictor categories are merged. Generally, CHAID uses the minimum of these two values to determine the best predictor. However, if the user has merged the predictor categories through the use of the Rearrange option, or if the specified minimum segment size has caused some categories to be merged that would not otherwise be merged, CHAID uses the adjusted *p* value computed after the categories are rearranged or the minimum segment size rule has taken effect. If all categories of the predictor are merged, the *p* value is set to 1. If no categories are merged, the unadjusted *p* value is used.

The unadjusted *p* value (labeled *prob* in CHAID output) is displayed at the bottom of the before-merge tables. The adjusted *p* value (labeled *adj. prob* in CHAID output) is displayed at the bottom of after-merge tables. The *p* value used by CHAID for determining the best predictor can be displayed using the Select option on the Tree menu. (To conserve space, *p* values are sometimes displayed using a shorthand notation. For example, $1.5 \times 10^{-64}$ may be displayed as $1.5e - 64$ or $1.5 - 64$.)

## Probabilities for Nominal Dependent Variables

Given a two-way table of observed cell counts $f_{ij}$, let $A$ denote the row (predictor) variable having $I$ categories and let $B$ denote the column (dependent) variable having

$J$ categories. CHAID considers each cell count in the two-way table to have arisen from the following saturated loglinear model (Haberman, 1978):

$$H_1\colon ln\,(\frac{F_{ij}}{Z_{ij}}) = \lambda + \lambda_i^A + \lambda_j^B + \lambda_{ij}^{AB}$$ **Equation B.1**

where $F_{ij}$ denotes the expected count for cell $(i, j)$ under some hypothesized model; $Z_{ij}$ equals $1/W_{ij}$, where $W_{ij}$ denotes the average sampling weight; and the lambda ($\lambda$) terms are model parameters that are subject to the usual identification conditions

$$\sum_i \lambda_i^A = \sum_j \lambda_j^B = 0$$ **Equation B.2**

and

$$\sum_i \lambda_{ij}^{AB} = \sum_j \lambda_{ij}^{AB} = 0$$ **Equation B.3**

Under the nominal method, the (unadjusted) $p$ value before categories are merged is the $p$ value associated with the null hypothesis of independence against the saturated alternative hypothesis $H_1$

$$H_0\colon \lambda_{ij}^{AB} = 0$$ **Equation B.4**

where $i$=1, 2,..., $I$; and $j$=1, 2,..., $J$.

Expected cell counts in CHAID are computed using the iterative proportional-fitting (IPF) algorithm (Deming & Stephan, 1940) modified to use the $Z_{ij}$ as starting values. This algorithm is known as the **weighted loglinear modeling (WLM) algorithm** (Magidson, 1987; Clogg & Eliasin, 1987).

If no weight variable is specified, each $Z_{ij}$ equals 1, the standard IPF algorithm is used, model $H_1$ becomes the more usual loglinear model representation (Goodman, 1978; Agresti, 1990), and the IPF algorithm will converge after a single iteration.

When weights are used, the WLM algorithm usually requires several iterations to achieve convergence. The convergence criterion is controlled by the epsilon and maximum iterations parameters (for more information on the technical settings, see "Technical" on p. 104). Convergence is achieved when certain estimated parameters change by less than epsilon from one iteration to the next. By default, the maximum number of iterations is 10, and epsilon is set to the special code "0" that makes epsilon proportional to the sample size for the current subgroup.

If the dependent variable is stratified (for example, if you use a 1% sample of nonresponders but 100% of responders and set one weight variable equal to 100 for nonresponders and another to 1 for responders), the WLM algorithm yields the same estimates for the expected counts as when no weights are used (Magidson, 1987; Clogg & Eliasin,

1987). Thus, you can speed up the analysis by turning off the WLM algorithm. However, in general, when sampling weights are used, turning off the WLM algorithm will yield incorrect estimates for the expected counts and $p$ values.

After convergence is achieved, a chi-square statistic is computed to assess the goodness of fit between the expected counts and the observed counts. By default, the likelihood-ratio chi-square statistic (labeled *LR Chi-square* in the output) is used. The likelihood-ratio statistic is equal to

$$L^2(H_0) = 2\sum_i \sum_j f_{ij} ln\left(\frac{f_{ij}}{\hat{F}_{ij}}\right)$$ **Equation B.5**

Alternatively, if you select the Pearson chi-square option, the following formula is used instead of Equation B.5:

$$X^2(H_0) = \sum_i \sum_j \frac{(f_{ij} - \hat{F}_{ij})^2}{\hat{F}_{ij}}$$ **Equation B.6**

The (unadjusted) $p$ value is then obtained from the chi-square distribution with degrees of freedom equal to $(I-1) \times (J-1)$. (CHAID actually estimates the logarithm of the $p$ value, so the estimate of the $p$ value itself is much more precise than usual.)

## Probabilities for Ordinal Dependent Variables

When you use the ordinal method, instead of testing the null hypothesis ($H_0$) of independence against the saturated alternative hypothesis ($H_1$), CHAID tests for independence against an unsaturated model, the Y association (or Y* association) model (Magidson, 1992, 1993a, 1993b)

$$H_1': ln\left(\frac{F_{ij}}{Z_{ij}}\right) = \lambda + \lambda_i^A + \lambda_j^B + x_i(y_j - \bar{y})$$ **Equation B.7**

where $y_j$ denotes the category score for the $j$th category of *B*, $x_i$ denotes unknown coefficients for the $y_j$, and $\bar{y}$ denotes the average score for the dependent variable.

In addition to the identification conditions in Equation B.2 and Equation B.3, the following identification condition on the $x$ parameters holds:

$$\bar{x} = 0$$ **Equation B.8**

where $\bar{x}$ denotes the average of the $x_i$.

Under model $H_1'$, the null hypothesis of independence becomes

$$H_0': x_1 = x_2 = \ldots = x_I \qquad \textbf{Equation B.9}$$

which is equivalent to

$$H_0'': (\mu_1 = \mu_2 = \ldots = \mu_I) \qquad \textbf{Equation B.10}$$

where

$$\mu_i = P_{i1}y_1 + P_{i2}y_2 + \ldots + P_{iJ}y_J \qquad \textbf{Equation B.11}$$

and $P_{ij}$ is the conditional probability of membership in category $j$ of $B$, given that an observation is classified within the $i$th category of $A$. For proof of the equivalence of Equation B.9 and Equation B.10, see Magidson (1992).

Estimation under the ordinal method involves two steps. In the first step, CHAID computes maximum-likelihood estimates for the expected cell counts under model $H_1'$. These counts preserve the Y association from the original table, but remove all other types of nonindependence. Then, these estimated counts are tested for independence using the following likelihood-ratio chi-square statistic:

$$L^2(H_0') = 2\sum_i\sum_j f'_{ij} ln\left(\frac{f'_{ij}}{\hat{F}_{ij}}\right) \qquad \textbf{Equation B.12}$$

where $f'_{ij}$ denotes the counts estimated under model $H_1'$ and $\hat{F}_{ij}$ denotes the expected counts estimated under independence (that is, under $H_0$). The actual degrees of freedom depend on the number of $y$ scores you prespecify.

Since all irrelevant sources of nonindependence are removed in the first step, this test uses fewer degrees of freedom and is thus more powerful than a test of independence. (The Pearson chi-square statistic is not available under the ordinal method.)

In the case that all of the $y_j$ in model $H_1'$ are prespecified, model $H_1'$ is equivalent to Goodman's row effects ($R$) model when the model is modified for unequal spacing (Goodman, 1979, 1985), and the general ordinal algorithm used by CHAID (Magidson, 1992) reduces to Goodman's maximum-likelihood algorithm. The degrees of freedom for the likelihood-ratio chi-square statistic in Equation B.12 are $I - 1$. Note that $I - 1$ represents the difference between the degrees of freedom under the independence model and the $R$ model:

$$(I-1)(J-1) - (I-1)(J-2) = I-1 \qquad \textbf{Equation B.13}$$

If all of the $y_j$ in model $H_1'$ are estimated using the CHAID calibration option with predictor $A$ as the instrument, model $H_1'$ is equivalent to Goodman's (1979) RC model and the algorithm again reduces to Goodman's iterative algorithm. The degrees of freedom in this case for assessing the likelihood-ratio chi-square statistic in Equation B.12 are $(I-1)+(J-2)$ for predictor *A* and $I-1$ for the other predictors.

If all the scores are estimated by calibration, CHAID employs a standardizing transformation so that the highest score is taken to be 100 and the lowest is 0. The user can use the Scale option to transform the calibrated scores so that the new score is 100 minus the old score—that is, a score of 100 is changed to 0 and 0 to 100.

Finally, in the case that at least one—but not all—of the $y$ scores is estimated with predictor *A* chosen as the instrument, the degrees of freedom for all predictors other than *A* are $I-1$. The degrees of freedom for predictor *A* will be set by CHAID to be

$$(I-1)+M$$ **Equation B.14**

where $M$ is the minimum of $J^*$ and $J-2$, and $J^* \le J$ denotes the number of scores that are estimated.

If $M$ is greater than 0, the degrees of freedom for testing the statistical significance for the predictor-*A* instrument will be higher than those for the other predictors to adjust for the fact that the estimation of the dependent variable scores are based on *A*. If this adjustment were not made, the degree of significance for *A* would be inflated.

A predictor is eligible for use as the instrument if the $I$-by-$J$ crosstabulation of the predictor by the dependent variable contains no more than $(I-1)\times(J-2)$ empty cells (cells containing no cases). If the predictor you select as the instrument contains too many empty cells, CHAID warns you that the selected predictor is not an eligible instrument. Generally, of all the predictors that are eligible, the one selected to be the instrument should be the one known to be associated with the dependent variable. For further interpretation of Equation B.7, see Goodman (1991).

You can control the number of iterations employed by the ordinal algorithm by altering the settings for the two technical parameters Epsilon and Maximum Iterations (see "Technical" on p. 104). Convergence is reached when certain estimated parameters are within epsilon of their theoretical maximum-likelihood solution, and a certain likelihood-ratio chi-square statistic is non-negative.

CHAID alerts you if convergence is not achieved and indicates which predictor is involved. After you click on Close to continue, if that variable for which convergence was not achieved happens to be the predictor used to split, you can increase the number of iterations (and/or lower the epsilon value) and repeat the analysis within the node that caused the message to determine whether the results differ. Otherwise, the convergence warning can be safely ignored. Or, if the convergence message appears during a calibration, you can increase the maximum number of iterations or change the epsilon value and recalibrate to determine whether the estimated scores change.

Finally, if a nonconvergence is encountered during automatic mode, CHAID warns you, at the end of the analysis, that at least one predictor was involved in a nonconvergence. After completion of the CHAID run, you can edit or print the log file to see that predictors were involved (the log file has the extension *.log* and uses the name of the current run as the prefix). Since CHAID's default settings for the maximum number of iterations and epsilon are conservative, in most cases you can ignore a nonconvergence message. If it is clear that the settings are too conservative for a given set of data, you can speed up the analysis and reduce the number of convergence warning messages by increasing the value of epsilon (for example, to 0.0015).

There are two reasons why convergence may not be achieved: either 1) after the maximum number of iterations has been reached, the deviation in parameter values is still greater than epsilon; or 2) epsilon is set too high and the likelihood-ratio chi-square statistic fails to take on a non-negative value. You may want to increase the number of iterations or lower the epsilon value and reanalyze the affected predictor (for more information on technical settings, see "Technical" on p. 104). The respective default values of 100 and 0.00015 should be sufficient for most data.

You can input any category scores for an ordinal dependent variable. If these scores are based on some predictor, the number of degrees of freedom used in the computation of predictor $p$ values should be adjusted. CHAID allows you to alter the number of degrees of freedom for some selected instrument by specifying the number of estimated scores technical parameter, $J^*$, and the predictor that you used as the instrument to derive these scores. Based on Equation B.14, CHAID will then determine the appropriate number of degrees of freedom for the instrument.

## Adjusted Probabilities

When two or more categories of the predictor variable have been merged together, either by the algorithm or manually through the use of the Rearrange option on the Tree menu, CHAID estimates a $p$ value by applying the preceding steps for the unadjusted $p$ value and then inflates the $p$ value by multiplying it by the Bonferroni multiplier $M^*$ (Kass, 1980).

The Bonferroni multiplier adjusts for the simultaneous inference associated with the fact that CHAID examines different ways to merge categories and selects the category merging that retains the most significance in the table. The Bonferroni adjustment is applied under both the nominal and ordinal methods of analysis.

For example, suppose that $A$ is a five-category free predictor that is dichotomized and that the nominal method is used. Let $\alpha$ denote the desired type 1 error rate associated with the test of independence in a two-way table formed by crosstabulating $A$ and $B$. (That is, $\alpha$ denotes the desired probability of rejecting the null hypothesis of independence when, in fact, independence holds.) Consider testing each of the 15 possible dichotomized forms for $B$. If these 15 tests were independent of each other, the probability of making a type 1 error in one or more of these tests is

$$1 - (1 - \alpha)^{15}$$ **Equation B.15**

which is substantially greater than $\alpha$. The probability in Equation B.15 is approximately $15\alpha$ when $\alpha$ is small. More generally, if $M^*$ equals the number of ways of ending up with $I' <= I$ categories, then we have the following for small $\alpha$:

$$1 - (1 - \alpha)^{M^*} = M^* \alpha$$ **Equation B.16**

Hence, if 15 tests are being performed, the $p$ value must be $\alpha/15$ or less to be considered significant at the $\alpha$ level.

For a free predictor,

$$M^* = \sum_{i=0}^{I'-1} (-1)^i \frac{(I'-i)^I}{i!\,(I'-i)!}$$ **Equation B.17**

For a monotonic predictor,

$$M^* = \begin{bmatrix} I-1 \\ I'-1 \end{bmatrix}$$ **Equation B.18**

For a float predictor,

$$M^* = \begin{bmatrix} I-1 \\ I'-1 \end{bmatrix} \left(\frac{I'-1+I'(I-I)}{I-1}\right)$$ **Equation B.19**

For example, under the nominal method, given that predictor *A* has $I'$ categories after merging, the unadjusted $p$ value will be that associated with $(I'-1) \times (J-1)$ degrees of freedom. This $p$ value is then multiplied by $M^*$, which is the number of ways in which *A* can obtain $I'$ categories when it originally had $I$ categories.

# Uniqueness of Estimated Scores

The relative distance between the scores is uniquely identified by the model. Let the superscript (*) distinguish those categories of the dependent variable for which a score is estimated. The relative distance between any three scores, say, $y^*_1$, $y^*_5$, and $y_3$, is defined as $(y^*_1 - y^*_5)/(y^*_5 - y_3)$.

The initial scores obtained from the CHAID score estimation algorithm may be transformed by any linear transformation without altering the relative distances between the scores. Without any loss in generality, CHAID uses a standard transformation with the calibration option that fixes the largest score at 100 and the lowest score at 0. Formally, we have

$$y'_j = 100\,(\hat{y}_j - \hat{y}_{MIN})\,/\,c \qquad \textbf{Equation B.20}$$

where $\hat{y}_{MIN}$ is the lowest initial estimate for the $y_j$ and $c$ is the highest initial estimate for the $y_j$ minus $\hat{y}_{MIN}$.

## Monotonic Calibration of the Dependent Variable

If the estimated category scores for an ordinal dependent variable are out of order, you can use the Smoothing option to combine categories so that the resulting scores are in order. CHAID uses two approaches for forming new categories that are properly ordered: the high-to-low method and the low-to-high method. Each method combines a category that is out of order with the previous category. CHAID derives estimated expected counts under both approaches and chi-squared statistics are computed to determine which method provides the better fit to the original observed counts. CHAID automatically selects the method that gives the closest fit to the observed data (that is, CHAID selects the maximum-likelihood solution).

The high-to-low method assumes that the correct ordering of scores is from high to low. Starting with the first two categories, CHAID checks to see if the order is correct. If not, the categories are merged and a new score for the merged category is computed as the weighted average of the original scores. If the original categories are ordered correctly, CHAID checks whether scores for the second and third categories are in correct order. If not, the categories are merged and again the score for the merged category is computed as the weighted average of the two scores that were out of order. The resulting score is then compared with the score of the previous category. If it is found to be out of order, it is again merged. The procedure continues in this manner until all category scores are properly ordered.

The low-to-high method works similarly except that a category is merged with the preceding category only if its score is lower.

If categories of the dependent variable are merged, either through the use of the smoothing option or by assigning the same score to two or more categories, the degrees of freedom will be based on the number of final categories of the dependent variable.

(You can use scaling to automatically reverse the calibrated scores whether or not the smoothing option is used.)

If smoothing is done, the resulting score estimates will not necessarily be maximum likelihood. To assure that the estimates are maximum likelihood, repeat the calibration a second time based on the new set of categories, which may include some combined categories (Agresti, 1987).

## Dichotomous Variables

For a dichotomous dependent variable, the nominal and ordinal methods yield identical *p* values (it does not matter whether the variable was originally dichotomous or dichotomized by deleting one or more categories, merging categories, or smoothing). The only difference between the nominal and ordinal methods is that the ordinal method displays the average score (rather than percentages) in tree nodes and in the table margins. (If the scores of 100 and 0 are assigned to the dependent variable categories, the average score is a percentage.)

For a dichotomous predictor variable, the *p* value is identical whether the variable is defined as a monotonic, free, or float variable.

# Appendix C
# Magazine Subscription Data

Table C.1 and Table C.2 describe variables in the magazine subscription data set used in the examples in this manual. The file (*subscrib.sav*) is an SPSS for Windows data file.

**Table C.1 Dependent variables in magazine subscription data set**

| Variable | | Category | |
|---|---|---|---|
| **Name** | **Label** | **Value** | **Label** |
| resp2 | Dichotomous Response (dichotomous variable) | 1 | Respondent |
| | | 2 | Nonrespondent |
| resp3 | Response to Sweep-stakes Promotion (trichotomous variable) | 1 | Paid Respondent |
| | | 2 | Unpaid Respondent |
| | | 3 | Nonrespondent |

**Table C.2 Predictor variables in magazine subscription data set**

| Variable | | Category | |
|---|---|---|---|
| **Name** | **Label** | **Value** | **Label** |
| age | Age of Household Head | 1 | 18–24 |
| | | 2 | 25–34 |
| | | 3 | 35–44 |
| | | 4 | 45–54 |
| | | 5 | 55–64 |
| | | 6 | 65+ |
| | | 7 | Unknown |
| gender | Sex of Household Head | 1 | Male |
| | | 2 | Female |
| kids | Known Presence of Children | 1 | Yes |
| | | 2 | No |

**Table C.2 Predictor variables in magazine subscription data set (Continued)**

| Variable | | Category | |
|---|---|---|---|
| **Name** | **Label** | **Value** | **Label** |
| income | Household Income (Estimated) | 1 | Under $8,000 |
| | | 2 | $8,000–$9,999 |
| | | 3 | $10,000–$14,999 |
| | | 4 | $15,000–$19,999 |
| | | 5 | $20,000–$24,999 |
| | | 6 | $25,000–$34,999 |
| | | 7 | $35,000–$49,999 |
| | | 8 | $50,000 or more |
| bankcard | Known Presence of Bankcard | 1 | Yes |
| | | 2 | No |
| hhsize | Number of Persons in Household | 1 | |
| | | 2 | |
| | | 3 | |
| | | 4 | |
| | | 5 | Five or more |
| | | 6 | Unknown |
| occup | Occupation of Household Head | 1 | White Collar |
| | | 2 | Blue Collar |
| | | 3 | Other |
| | | 4 | Unknown |

# Appendix D
# The R-squared Statistic

The $R$-squared ($R^2$) statistic in the original release of CHAID is not available in the current version because the statistic may be misleading when used with categorical dependent variables.

For example, consider the dichotomous dependent variable *resp2* with 1000 responders and 99,000 nonresponders. Suppose that a dichotomous predictor variable called *segment* produces two equal-sized segments (*A* and *B*), as shown in Table D.1.

**Table D.1 Table of segment by resp2**

| | Responders | Nonresponders | Total |
|---|---|---|---|
| **Segment A** | 0 | 50,000 | 50,000 |
| **Segment B** | 1000 | 49,000 | 50,000 |
| **Total** | 1000 | 99,000 | 100,000 |

The response rate is 0% for *segment A* and 2% for *segment B*. *Segment* is a highly significant predictor. (The chi-square statistic is 1396 with one degree of freedom.) In fact, *segment* is the best possible predictor among predictors that divide the sample into two equal groups.

The regression $R^2$ statistic for this example is 0.01, indicating that only 1% of the variance in *resp2* is explained by *segment*. If you look at only the $R^2$ statistic, you might conclude that *segment* is not a good predictor of *resp2*. (For the formula for computing $R^2$ for a categorical dependent variable, see Magidson, 1981.)

The reason for the low $R^2$ value is that the marginal distributions for *resp2* and *segment* are very different. *Resp2* is heavily skewed toward nonresponse, while *segment* is distributed equally between the segments. Given these marginal distributions, the maximum possible value for $R^2$ is 0.01.

Of course, in the special case where two variables have a bivariate normal distribution, both marginal distributions are normal and neither variable will be skewed. In this case, the maximum correlation of 1.0 can be obtained. However, in general, the maximum correlation of 1.0 can be obtained only if the variables have exactly the same marginal distribution. The $p$-value used by CHAID to assess significance is not affected by marginal distributions.

# Appendix E
# Additional Tree Diagram Output

When output is directed to either the Clipboard or a File via the Print/Clipboard dialog box, the Tree Diagram selection causes text information to be generated. (Note that when output is directed to the Clipboard, two formats are available.) This text information consists of one line of data for each node in the tree diagram. If the Headings box is checked, the first line contains field names. The fields in the data line are shown in Table E.1.

**Table E.1 Data line fields**

| No. | Name | Description |
|---|---|---|
| 1 | Node | An integer, starting with 1, which uniquely identifies each node. |
| 2 | Parent | The node ID of the node (above the current node) to which the current node is attached. |
| 3 | Depth | The number of levels between this node and the top of the tree. |
| 4 | X | An arbitrary horizontal coordinate value that locates the node in a graphic diagram. |
| 5 | Y | An arbitrary vertical coordinate value that locates the node in a graphic diagram. |
| 6 | Catn | The category number of the current node (the variable is identified in the parent node). |
| 7 | Ncat | The total number of categories (the variable is identified in the parent node). |
| 8 | Category | The string of symbols that appears in the tree diagram. |
| 9 | Variable | The variable name selected for this node. For terminal nodes, or segments, the form "-m-" appears instead, where "m" is the segment number that appears in the gains chart. |
| 10 | Score | The score value that appears in the gains chart. |
| 11 | Total | The weighted total count for this node. |
| 12 | Count1 | The weighted total count for category 1 of the dependent variable. |
| 13 | Count2 | The weighted total count for category 2 of the dependent variable. |
| ... | Count | Repeated as needed for each category of the dependent variable. |

A sample of the output is shown in Table E.2.

**Table E.2 Tree diagram output**

| ID | Parent | Depth | X | Y | Catn | Ncat | Category | Variable | Score | Total | Count1 | Count2 |
|---|---|---|---|---|---|---|---|---|---|---|---|---|
| 1 | 0 | 1 | 213 | 27 | 0 | 0 | “<Total>” | “hhsize” | 1.14882 | 81040 | 931 | 80109 |
| 2 | 1 | 2 | 129 | 57 | 1 | 4 | “1” | “-1-” | 1.0873 | 25384 | 276 | 25108 |
| 3 | 1 | 2 | 185 | 57 | 2 | 4 | “23” | “occup” | 1.52492 | 16132 | 246 | 15886 |
| 4 | 3 | 3 | 157 | 87 | 1 | 2 | “W” | “-2-” | 2.38908 | 1758 | 42 | 1716 |
| 5 | 3 | 3 | 199 | 87 | 2 | 2 | “B-.” | “bankcard” | 1.41923 | 14374 | 204 | 14170 |
| 6 | 5 | 4 | 185 | 117 | 1 | 2 | “Y” | “-3-” | 2.00547 | 2194 | 44 | 2150 |
| 7 | 5 | 4 | 213 | 117 | 2 | 2 | “N” | “-4-” | 1.31363 | 12180 | 160 | 12020 |
| 8 | 1 | 2 | 241 | 57 | 3 | 4 | “4F” | “-5-” | 1.91997 | 6198 | 119 | 6079 |
| 9 | 1 | 2 | 283 | 57 | 4 | 4 | “.” | “gender” | 0.870191 | 33326 | 290 | 33036 |
| 10 | 9 | 3 | 269 | 87 | 1 | 2 | “M” | “-6-” | 0.806862 | 25531 | 206 | 25325 |
| 11 | 9 | 3 | 297 | 87 | 2 | 2 | “F” | “-7-” | 1.07761 | 7795 | 84 | 7711 |

This text information is similar to the *.his* file produced by the original version of CHAID and can be used as input to your own custom “tree drawing” or other graphical display program.

# Bibliography


Agresti, A. 1984. *Analysis of ordinal categorical data*. New York: John Wiley and Sons.

_____. 1987. Order-restricted score parameters in association models for contingency tables. *Journal of the American Statistical Association*, 82: 619–623.

_____. 1990. *Categorical data analysis*. New York: John Wiley and Sons.

Clogg, C. C., and S. R. Eliasin. 1987. Some common problems in log-linear analysis. *Sociological Methods and Research*, 16:1, 8–44.

Deming, W. E., and F. F. Stephan. 1940. On a least squares adjustment of a sampled frequency table when the expected marginal totals are known. *Annals of Mathematical Statistics*, 11: 427–444.

Derrick, F., and J. Magidson. 1992. Using CHAID with the gains chart option. In: *Proceedings of the 1992 Annual Meeting of the American Statistical Association*, Business and Economics Section.

Goodman, L. A. 1978. *Analyzing qualitative/categorical data*, J. Magidson, ed. Cambridge, Mass.: Abt Books.

_____. 1979. Simple models for the analysis of associations in cross-classifications having ordered categories. *Journal of the American Statistical Association*, 74: 537–552.

_____. 1984. Simple models for the analysis of associations in cross-classifications having ordered categories. In: *The analysis of cross-classified data having ordered categories*. Cambridge, Mass.: Harvard University Press.

_____. 1985. The analysis of cross-classified data having ordered and/or unordered categories: Association models, correlation models, and asymmetry models for contingency tables with or without missing entries. *The Annals of Statistics*, 13:1, 10–69.

_____. 1991. Measures, models and graphic displays in the analysis of cross-classified data. *Journal of the American Statistical Association*, 86: 1085–1138.

Grizzle, J. E., C. F. Starmer, and G. G. Koch. 1969. Analysis of categorical data by linear models. *Biometrics*, 25: 489–504.

Haberman, S. 1978. *Analysis of qualitative data*. Vol. 1: Introductory topics. New York: Academic Press.

Kass, G. 1980. An exploratory technique for investigating large quantities of categorical data. *Applied Statistics*, 29:2, 119–127.

Magidson, J. 1981. Variance, entropy and correlation ratios for nominal dependent variables. *Social Science Research*, 10: 177–194.

_____. 1982. Some common pitfalls in causal analysis of categorical data. *Journal of Marketing Research*, 19: 460–471.

_____. 1987. Weighted log-linear modeling. In: *1987 Proceedings of the Social Statistics Division*, American Statistical Association, 171–174.

_____. 1988. Improved statistical techniques for response modeling: Progression beyond regression. *Journal of Direct Marketing*, 2:4, 6–18.

_____. 1989. CHAID, LOGIT and log-linear modeling. *Marketing Information Systems, Report 11-130*. Delran, N.J.: Datapro Research Corporation.

_____. 1992. Chi-squared analysis of a scalable dependent variable. In: *Proceedings of the 1992 Annual Meeting of the American Statistical Association*, Educational Statistics Section.

_____. 1993a. The CHAID approach to segmentation modeling. In: *Handbook of Marketing Research*, R. Bagozzi, ed. Cambridge, Mass.: Blackwell.

_____. 1993b. The use of the new ordinal algorithm in CHAID to target profitable segments. *Journal of Database Marketing*, 1:1.

# Index